W9-AED-598

PL SEP 2022

Faith Is the Victory

Faith Is the Victory

by
BUELL H. KAZEE

Bible Teacher, Lexington Baptist College
Lexington, Kentucky

LEXINGTON BAPTIST COLLEGE
Lexington, Kentucky

FAITH IS THE VICTORY
by Buell H. Kazee

Copyright, 1951, *by*
Wm. B. Eerdmans Publishing Company
All rights in this book are reserved. No part may be reproduced
in any manner without permission in writing from the publisher,
except brief quotations used in connection with a review in a
magazine or newspaper.

Set up and printed, January, 1951

Second printing, March, 1954

PRINTED IN THE UNITED STATES OF AMERICA

Introduction

From the day that God opened the gates of Eden He has been calling men to a life of faith. Grace is, and ever has been, God's way of saving all men who come to Him. Law, and the covenant with Israel, were God's instruments by which He made His people conscious of sin and drove them to the Saviour.

The Bible teaches, in summary, three great truths: first, God alone is holy; second, man is sinful, depraved, and lost; and third, Jesus is the only Saviour.

The whole Book of books is a revelation of these three great truths, and the Hero of the entire Book is Jesus. Man can but fall at His feet and adore Him. Any preaching or teaching that does not at last bring us to that position is contrary to the entire revelation of God to us.

There are only two philosophies of salvation in the world: salvation by works, and salvation by grace. It matters not in what variety of forms they come, nor under what names or heads they are expressed, they are ever the same; and the one is wholly contrary to the other.

God creates man in His image, and man creates God in his image. It depends on who is doing the creating as to what kind of being we have in either case. Man, left to himself, will always have a god; and that god will always be like himself. Because man is confused, he will make for himself many gods, but they will all be like himself. The conflict of the world is between the One God who arises from out yonder beyond man's realm of knowledge, and the many gods which he has created out of his own heart.

Man's gods originate from the inspiration of Satan, another deity, who holds sway over the mind of man. God's proposal is to attract man from his many gods to the One God. This requires a display of miracle on the part of God — a display of power and wisdom unknown to man. That is the purpose of miracle. Therefore, the God of miracle is our only hope.

As the ages have moved along we find it has been easy for those, who have come to know the true God, to lose sight of Him while walking in this world, and to become occupied for periods of time by the gods of this world. These periods we have known as periods of backsliding on the part of God's people.

This is commonly known among us as "worldliness." It may be termed accurately as "the works of the flesh." It may take two general forms: (1) It may be open rebellion and sinful practice as recognized by all. (2) It may be a conscientious act of reliance upon the flesh to accomplish God's ends. The latter is much more subtle than the former, and is the place where Satan most often deceives the followers of Christ.

Believers who turn to the world in open sin against God are, most often, babes in Christ who are victims of weakness in the flesh, and who lack the help which more mature believers should be constantly giving. But those who are most likely to be deceived, and those whom Satan seeks most to deceive, are those zealous and conscientious souls who earnestly want to serve God. Here is where the battle is pitched, and here you will find Satan trying to occupy the land.

To supplant God in His own territory, to divert energies and devotion of God's people to a useless end, and, without their knowing it, to make them believe they are working in the Spirit when they are actually working in the energies of the flesh, these are the methods of Satan. He would counterfeit God and steal our devotion.

His whole purpose is to reshape God in our minds, and by this subtle method make of Him a God who must be served rather than a God who can serve us. He proposes to get us to show our devotion to God by devising many things for us to do for Him, all of which may be good, rather than to let us submit ourselves to that God in order that He may do great things for us. The result is that we are to parade before the world a tabulated, blackboard analysis of how much we love Him, rather than acknowledge our terrible need and see Him perform His miracles of love for us in transforming us into His likeness. In the former *we* get the glory of a human accomplishment, and the world is not impressed because it is mere competition with what the world has to offer; in the latter *God* gets the glory of an exclusively divine accomplishment, and the world is impressed because they have seen "the Lord's doings, and it is marvelous in" their eyes.

In this book we want to return to that God who does things for us, and who, by His matchless deeds for us, makes sinners dissatisfied with the gods they have, and thus impels them to turn to Him.

In so doing we will find that this God does His work in a manner wholly contrary to the manner of the flesh; so that God's ways will look foolish to the wisdom of the flesh; and, in so doing, His work will appear to be miraculous, and thus destroy the self-sufficiency which has so often supplanted the power of God in our lives.

7

Our device for teaching these great truths is the pilgrimage of God's chosen people, the Israelites, from Egypt to Canaan. A brief sketch of the design will be sufficient, but it will be necessary before we enter upon the message of this book. After having shown how the God of Abraham, Isaac, and Jacob has done marvelous things for His people in every age, we shall endeavor to show how the faith principle works in our personal lives, and how the believer may enter into the "VICTORY THAT OVERCOMES THE WORLD, EVEN OUR FAITH."

Contents

Faith Is the Victory

CHAPTER I

The Pattern of the Christian's Life

THE PATTERN of the Christian's life is laid down in symbol in the journey of God's people from Egypt to the Promised Land. It is divided into three general phases: (1) From Egypt to Kadesh-barnea, representing a period of education of the believer under the special direction of God. (2) From Kadesh-barnea to the river Jordan, which represents a phase of disciplinary experience in which God deals with the self life. (3) The conquest of Canaan, which represents the life of victory through faith.

This book is concerned with the last phase of this great experience, its application to the church life of God's people and to their lives as individuals.

In this journey the life of the believer is *dramatically* portrayed. In Paul's *Letter to the Romans* the life of the believer is *theologically* expounded. The same message is set forth in both. Thus, the Apostle in I Corinthians 10:11 says: "Now these things happened unto them for ensamples; and they are written for our admonition, upon whom the ends of the world are come." Here, and other places in God's Word, we are told that God has recorded in the history of His chosen people, the Israelites, the great truths which we need to guide us and empower us along our pilgrimage here on earth.

The reader would do well to review the account of this great journey, and note how utterly dependent upon God were His people, and how the incidents along the way give that marvelous display of divine grace in behalf of an unworthy people, simply because somebody believed God. Since many others have led us with such great profit along this pathway, and have pointed out with such diligent observation the wonderful truths revealed in this journey of symbolic teaching, we shall content ourselves with a simple restatement of the symbolism, and press on to where our message begins.

Egypt represents the bondage of sin in which all of us are born. The passover lamb is a type of Christ our Saviour, the "lamb slain from the foundation of the world" (Rev. 13:8).

The blood applied to the door posts represents the sinner's trust in Christ to save, while the baptism at the Red Sea depicts the experience actualized in the sinner's heart. The former represents a transaction recorded on the book of God in Heaven when He pronounces the sinner justified by faith; the latter represents the experiential realization of this faith in the sinner's heart through the Holy Ghost who comes in to dwell. (Note: No attempt is here made to separate these two phases of "conversion" by time and sequence).

This is the sense in which the Holy Ghost baptizes us into the death and resurrection of Christ. This is not the so-called "baptism of the Holy Ghost," but is rather that baptism spoken of by Paul in Romans 6:3, 4: "Know ye not that so many of us as were baptized into Jesus Christ were baptized into his death? Therefore we are buried with him by baptism into death; that like as Christ was raised up from the dead by the glory of the Father, even so we also should walk in newness of life."

Thus, the child of God, by death, is cut off from the world and pronounced dead to sin. Thus, also, he is raised up from the dead and made alive unto Christ, and is ready now to begin his walk as a believer, a child of God.

Now the child of God is on his way to the Promised Land, singing with Miriam, Moses' sister, "Sing ye to the Lord, for he hath triumphed gloriously; the horse and the rider he hath thrown into the sea" (Ex. 15:22).

The events which follow in the next few weeks are full of teaching, but we must leave this to other studies. We should like to repeat that all these events up to Kadesh-barnea were educational and were designed by the Lord Himself to instruct His children in the ways of God, as well as to wean them from the life in Egypt. At Sinai they camp for a while to learn the three great truths which we have indicated in the introduction: (1) That man is utterly sinful. (2) That God is utterly holy. (3) That Jesus is the only Saviour. The first two of these great truths are taught through the Ten Commandments; the third is taught through the tabernacle and the offerings.

At last they are brought, by a varied pathway, to Kadesh-barnea, where God offers to give them the Promised Land if they will believe. Their unbelief closes the gate to this great experience, and they begin the *second phase* of this journey, the wilderness wanderings. During this period all those who were twenty years old when they left Egypt, except Caleb and Joshua, died. This is a type of the destruction of the flesh, as we have said, and represents that experience in the life of the believer which is described in Romans 7, the flesh warring against the Spirit. Thus

God designed to get rid of that unbelieving group which
hindered the spiritual progress of Israel. It took the Israelites, because of this one act of unbelief, thirty-eight
years to come to what might have been reached in a few
days, had they believed God and marched in by faith.
So it is that God lets us, who lean upon the arm of flesh,
wander in the wilderness of our own fleshly wisdom and
carnality until we come at last, in desperation perhaps, to
that point where we see that we must *live* by faith just as
we were *saved* by faith. This is the spiritual mystery which
we seek to recapture and make real to the reader in this
message. All too often it requires too much time and sad
experience for us to mature, to learn to trust, to rely blindly
upon God's Word, and to get through with the temptation
to rely upon the flesh. Too often we come late in life, if
ever at all, to the great achievements wrought by faith. It
takes so long for self to die out!

So without discussing the details, we would say that the
wilderness wanderings represent the life of the carnal Christian, the babe in Christ, delayed and stinted in his growth.
When we follow the direction of this course we find that
they just wandered around, here and there, without any direct objective. Once again, it seems, they came to Kadesh-
barnea and looked with weary longing into the Promised
Land. Yea, they even tried to take it in the strength of the
flesh, but were defeated. Their experiences with heathen nations involved them time and again, and in nearly every case
they become despised rather than glorified. It is always true
with those who try to play with the world and belong to
God at the same time. They have just enough religion to
keep them miserable, to make them despised by the world
and pitied by the righteous.

Carnal living is the poorest of all kinds of living. "Wishy-washy" is the common coinage for it. Babes in fretful mood, always crying out for something for self, complaining that they do not get any joy out of their religion! Not only do they become cares and burdens to pastors and spiritual leaders, demanding to be wheeled about in baby carriages and fed on sugar stick diets, but at last they get big enough to lust for the flesh pots of Egypt and are easily led astray by the mixed multitudes in the world about them. They want the church fashioned after their tastes and built after a world order. They want to indulge in worship that will produce a mystic spell over their fleshy religious nature and make it "feel good."

Out of this carnality has grown much of the busy life of the modern church. The flesh is terribly religious, and through it Satan works his greatest deception, making the carnal one feel that he is deeply religious while working in the energy of the flesh.

The glory of Israel among heathen nations was always a display of what God could do for a people who were His for a possession. God was always the big attraction. Israel was merely a people chosen of God as the body of flesh through which He could manifest Himself to the world. When they trusted in Him and let Him do great things for them, the heathen were impressed and God was glorified. But the modern church, the body through which and on behalf of which God meant to demonstrate His power to the world and thus attract the lost unto Himself, has substituted its own works for His, and set up, after a world order, a great business institution in an attempt to impress the world.

If God *should* succeed through our great promotional organizations, He would get little or no credit for it, for, according to the world's estimate, the set-up we have ought to succeed anyway. It has all the expertness of the world in it — organization, efficiency, method, psychology, psychiatry, learning, culture, world appeal, and all that it takes to be successful after the wisdom of the flesh. If it should succeed it would be apparent that we, not God, did it. All this is the product of the carnal mind.

But, as Paul says, "Behold, I show you a better way." In the first chapter of Joshua we find Israel poised on the banks of Jordan, about to enter the Promised Land. Over and over again Moses reminds the people, "Now don't forget *what God has done for you*." Then he repeats the exploits of God in miracles performed before their very eyes. This is the kind of preaching we need today, telling what God has done for us. He summarizes the law, "thou shalt love the Lord thy God," and in every possible way warns them against any god but the ONE GOD.

Let us here observe that idolatry is the outstanding sin of man. Another god is always the devil's temptation. Do something else, have something else, be something else, always something else beside what God says. A supplanter, that is Satan. He would always occupy us with something else, another god. That is the one thing God cannot tolerate.

Joshua is the example of absolute surrender. Moses and the law have had their day. Across Jordan lies a land which can be conquered by faith alone, and Joshua is the man to lead them there. The crossing of Jordan sets forth the act of surrender of life, or, as we commonly say, "consecration" or "dedication." It is turning from reliance upon the wisdom of the flesh to complete trust in the "foolishness" of God. The carnal man has had his day. We come now to the maturity which Paul identifies as the "spiritual man."

Note carefully here, spirituality is not necessarily being good; it is, rather, coming into a spiritual understanding. It is a secret of grace, so plain and simple when seen, but so dark and complex when not seen. Sometimes believers grasp it immediately upon conversion; in others it comes later in life; but many of God's children never discover it. It is simply, as we may often repeat, finding out that we can no more live our lives in our own strength and wisdom than we can thus save ourselves. It is coming to *live* by faith just as we are *saved* by faith.

Before Israel crossed Jordan they had to deal with a special neglect of life in the wilderness; that is, the neglect of the life of separation which was symbolized in the act of circumcision. This sign of the covenant made with Abraham had been neglected, and now, before they could enter the land, they must clear away this reproach by circumcising all who had not been circumcised.

This neglect is a symbol of world conformity in the church of this day. If there is any one thing which God required of His people above another, it is that they be separate, not only from the world, but unto Him. There must not only be allegiance to God, but there must be no allegiance to any other. Of course, modern Christianity has another view of this matter. Religious leaders of today often feel that if we will be similar enough to the world so as not to embarrass it, the world will want to come in and add to our numbers. And so it will, only it will want to bring into our midst its heathen gods and customs and compromise our allegiance to our God. That is what has happened in the modern church. The result is that we have had to build a religious program that will please that world mind, but minus the power of God. This will be more apparent as we continue.

Certainly the Israelites could not hope to see God manifest His powers in her behalf as long as she remained in this state of neglect and world conformity. The covenant with Abraham must be honored if God was to work in their behalf. And if we are to enter into absolute surrender, to know the power and blessing of the life of faith, certainly separation from the world is our first imperative. We can never cross Jordan without saying good-bye to our reliance upon the flesh. The warfare over there is the "good fight of faith."

It is now the season of Jordan's overflow, the harvest time, but that does not matter. God must open the way, and it does not matter if the water be shallow or deep. As soon as the feet of the priests touched the water, Jordan rolled back into a great wall above and dried up below. As soon as the entire people had passed over, one man from each tribe set up a stone in the midst of the river, as a memorial that the old Israel, which had striven under law and in the energy of the flesh to reach their goal, was now dead. The Jordan rolled over that memorial. But these same twelve men took other twelve stones and set them up on the other side of Jordan, as a memorial to the new Israel which now begins to walk by faith and not by sight. From now on they are not to be concerned about what they can do, but with what they can trust God to do for them. So, the believer comes to that time when he sees the failure of the flesh and gives up the whole battle to God, saying: "Lord, I now bury the wisdom of the flesh in Jordan. I raise a new memorial on the side of faith, by which I declare that I have a new and spiritual understanding of the Christian life. No longer will I be concerned about what self wants, but about what Christ wants. When I pray I will not always be asking things for my comfort and convenience but rather I will be seeking a place in God's will and asking for grace to stand where God wants me. I will not strive to show my love for God by the efforts of the flesh, but rather by the worship and trust of my heart. I will no longer try to show what great things I can do for Him, but will yield myself to Him so that He can show the world what great things He can do for me." This is what it means to surrender our lives to Christ, and the crossing of Jordan is the symbolic portrayal of that surrender.

What, then, is the Promised Land? It is not a type of Heaven. "I Am Bound for the Promised Land" is a treasured old song, but it does not present the truth about the Promised Land. For, instead of

> *"All o'er those wide extended plains*
> *Shines one eternal day;*
> *There God the Son forever reigns,*
> *And scatters night away,"*

we have a land inhabited by heathen nations, fortified and protected by warlike giants who do not intend to yield one inch to invaders. It is not theirs, but the land which God gave to Abraham and his seed forever; yet it has been usurped and occupied by the enemies of God. It represents that realm of our lives which has been usurped and occupied by Satan, and which God proposes to subdue and recapture. We could not rout the enemy and repossess our lives in the strength and wisdom of the flesh. So now we come to take it in the strength and wisdom of God, and we are asked to believe and see Him do it for us.

To those who take their stand on faith, God says, as He did to Joshua, "See, I have given into thine hand Jericho" (Josh. 6:2). "Every place that the sole of your foot shall tread upon, that have I given unto you, as I said unto Moses" (Josh. 1:3). Then in the 9th verse He says, "Be strong and of good courage; be not afraid, neither be thou dismayed: for the Lord thy God is with thee, whithersoever thou goest."

CHAPTER II

Faith at Work

BEFORE we attempt to attack the walled cities in our individual lives, we want to know if faith works. Will our God, to whom we have surrendered all things, work for us as we believe and trust Him? Can we turn from all fleshly resources and depend entirely upon Him to do for us what we have been striving to do in the flesh? The answer to these questions lies in the record of heroes of faith. We cannot review all of them, but we shall select a few in whose behalf God has so ably demonstrated His power.

In these demonstrations many important truths will appear, but we are concerned mainly with these four:

1. We need to return to the God who can do something for us. We have left this God and have turned to the cold-hearted idols of self-sufficiency which we have carved out with our own hands. The miracle of religion is almost gone. We must go back to the God of miracle and power.

2. If we submit to Him to do for us what we are striving and failing to do in the flesh, we will find that His methods of work are wholly different from ours. Since "my ways are not your ways," and since "as the heavens are higher than the earth so are my ways higher than your ways," His methods will often seem foolish to us. For, "the foolishness of God is wiser than men, and the weakness of God

is stronger than men." It is "not by might nor by power, but by my Spirit, saith the Lord."

3. We will find that what attracts men to God is "the Lord's doings," not ours. When God is on display the people will come to Him and believe; but they will not be moved by the works of our hands for God.

4. The choicest faith is that which believes when there is no sign to encourage, except the Word of God.

Paul says that *we* are justified by our faith; but James says our *faith* is justified by our works. So, the question is, can faith do anything? Not, can *we* do anything, but can our *faith* do anything? Does faith really work? If so, what does it do? And the answer is, it brings us into that state of utter dependence upon God where God can show His power in our behalf. As long as we try to accomplish our ends in the strength and wisdom of the flesh, God cannot work. It is when we put the responsibility of it all upon Him that He responds with His matchless power. Does the record of God bear out this truth?

Now let us call a few witnesses who will assure us that our God can work for us.

JOSHUA

The Israelites face Jericho, a city walled and fortified beyond all power of the chosen people to penetrate its walls. They are now at war with the enemies of God. I have seen many people who thought that when we surrender our lives to God our troubles will then be over, and we shall find a calm, peaceful existence from there on. By all means, no! This is the day when we cease to be babes in Christ and become soldiers of the cross. Israel has been a babe in the wilderness; now the new era dawns: they become soldiers marching to conquer a land inhabited by the strongest and most warlike tribes of the earth. The war has just begun for the believer who makes complete surrender.

But it is a new kind of fighting, with a different kind of result. In I Timothy 6:12, Paul says: "Fight the good fight of faith." Paul had fought a good fight. But it was the good fight of faith. The battle of faith is a struggle, not to do, but to believe that God will do; to gain the ground of faith when, from all earthly evidence, it looks impossible that a promise can be fulfilled. The battle is always pitched on the question, "Can I believe exactly what God says?"

When Jesus came down off the mount of transfiguration He met a man with a demon-possessed son, who told the sad story that the disciples had been unable to do anything for him. The man said, "If thou canst do anything . . . help us" (Mark 9:22). In substance, Jesus answered, "As to what I can do, that is settled; the question is, can you believe?" Here is the fight of faith set forth concretely. Can I believe what God says? And that challenge comes to the believer every day. If we could believe, what wonders might God perform! But we lose the battle on faith. If we can win there, we have the victory.

Joshua is preparing to attack a walled city. His army is a straggling group of unfit, undisciplined, unarmed, very poor fighting men. All military aspects have faded from Israel, for, as we have noted, the fighting men which started from Egypt, who would not believe, died in the wilderness. There can now be no reliance upon the resources of the flesh. How can they attack this heavily fortified and important city?

Dramatically, a figure steps out of the shadows (Josh. 5:13-15). That figure has in his hand a drawn sword.

Joshua is very alert and wants to know who he is. "Do you come as a friend or an enemy?" he queries. "I come as the captain of the Lord's host," said the figure, with a modesty that puts Joshua into the dust. Joshua is a surrendered man and knows how to act. If in his own mind he ever bore the title "Captain," it was a relief to his anxious heart to transfer it immediately to the figure before him.

I wonder what might have been our feeling had we been in Joshua's place. I do not decry or belittle the honest efforts put forth by our churches today to improve and better prepare our membership for service. But I cannot help wondering what might have taken place here if Joshua had been a modern expert in plans and methods of church work. He might have said: "Well, indeed, I am glad you have come along; we shall need you. However, you are a little early. We have much to do before we are ready to attack.

"You see, Jericho is no mean city. Its citizens are modern in their life and customs. They are cultured and educated and very efficient in their way of life. Our people are just out of the wilderness, and they cannot, in their condition, hope to make any appeal to a city like Jericho. We must set up our tabernacle here, but we must make many changes. We must study the most modern ways of life as lived in Jericho and must revamp our whole system to meet their needs, so that we may not insult their intelligence. Our people are poorly prepared to do this. All they know of religious life is the old out-moded system of sacrifices and offerings, and we have been over and over it again, doing the same things, saying the same things, singing the same old songs, until we are ourselves worn out with its monotony. Jericho is a city of great musical talent and art and culture. Our system would make no appeal to them.

"Besides, our tabernacle is not adequate. A complete change in plan of it must be devised and larger and better accomodations must be provided. New ideas of form and ceremony must be introduced to bring us up to date. We must see how they worship inside the wall and incorporate the best ideas in our own worship. Furthermore, our people must be trained to greet and welcome those who may come to us as well as how to go after them. There is much latent talent in Jericho, which, if we can capture it for the Lord, will be a great asset to us. And they have great wealth there, too, and if we can capture their hearts, their money will go to honor God instead of to their heathen idols.

"Now, this cannot be done hastily. We must train and train and train, until we can meet them on their own basis. We must send overtures of friendship to them and let them see that we are not their enemies, but their friends. Through kindness and understanding we shall seek their friendship, and we are sure that it will not be long until they will open their gates to us. We will continue visiting them and mingling with them in friendliness until we have won their esteem. Then we will arrange some social life in our tabernacle which will be very much like the things they do. On a few occasions we will invite them to meet with us and enjoy our good, wholesome, social life with us.

"Of course, we must have our groups and ages so organized as to make any of them feel at home among us, and to let them take part in our meetings so that they will feel that it is their tabernacle as well as ours.

"We must not speak of them as heathen, or sinners, nor offend them by making them feel that they are any worse than are we. That will require leaders who are trained in the most modern methods of psychology, who

can deal with situations tactfully. After we have established
a friendship with them, we will take a census and enumerate
the prospects. When all has been classified and set up for
them, we will go among them personally and urge them
to come with us.

"But if we do not have our work well organized and
running with great efficiency, we will lose them; for that
is the way they do things in their city. We must remember
that they have great talents which we can use for God,
and great wealth. They can be a great asset to our communion. When we have gained access to the city, we will
doubtless find many ideas among the leaders of Jericho
which will be of inestimable value to us. We want to consult their psychologists and psychiatrists especially, and
learn the temper of their people.

"We are to have a meeting of our tribal heads in a day
or so, and they will lay plans for all this work. You see,
we want them to understand that we have not come to tear
down their city nor to destroy their way of life, but that
we have come to give them also the added blessings of our
God. In this we feel we can do a great service for our
God.

"When we have the final plans drawn up, and our forces
efficiently organized, we hope you will give us your blessing
and move with us into the campaign. We are sure that
with your assistance our work will so appeal to the citizens
of Jericho that we will take the entire city for God, and we
will all come out of this great venture with victory, *and
without a scratch!*"

I know this is satire, but I plead before my Lord a sincere motive. I know also that this is not the spirit of all
who lead in the plans and methods of modern church life.

I do not decry everything we do. It is the emphasis I am deploring. And, with so much to do in plans and method, it is well nigh impossible for us to avoid looking to our efficiency as our hope of winning the lost. The point I am making is that we are afraid to trust the unworldly, "slow and awkward" ways of our God. That is why I say that, from all world viewpoints, our plans should succeed whether God is in them or not, because they are so efficient.

Joshua, a man of faith, knew a different way. When God stands with sword drawn, it is time to bow down. So, like a surrendered soul, walking entirely by faith, and fighting to believe in spite of the way things looked, he said through lips that kissed the earth, "What saith my Lord to his servant?" If anybody in Israel thought Joshua was captain, it was not Joshua. How that ought to wither the great outlay of distinctions which we have borrowed from the world!

"And the captain of the Lord's host said unto Joshua, Loose thy shoe from off thy foot; for the place whereon thou standest is holy. And Joshua did so."

Worship! that is what God wants. That is what He must have if we are going to see Him fight our battles for us. *Brother W. T. Connor of the Southwestern Baptist Seminary rightly says in one of his books what we have said in substance for years, that the first business of the church is worship. And, to worship God is to resign from all fleshly resources, confess our impotence, and look to Him. It is not merely putting God first, but rather making Him everything.

As far as God was concerned the action had already been taken. "See," He says, "I have given into thy hand Jeri-

---

* Now deceased.

cho, and the king thereof, and the mighty men thereof."
Then He unfolded to Joshua HIS plan! Yes! God has
plans! But they are always contrary to the plans of the
world mind. Not a military man in the world would have
looked upon God's suggestions as being anything but utter
foolishness. And that is exactly what God thinks of our
plans. For, "the foolishness of God is wiser than men; and
the weakness of God is stronger than men" (I Cor. 1:25).
Is it not so!

I can imagine that the spectacle of Israel's army was
indeed puzzling to the world's best military men of that
day upon the wall. Perhaps they said: "What strange
aggregation is that which approaches our city? Surely they
cannot be men of war planning to attack us. See, in the
forefront there are seven men dressed like leaders of some
tribal ceremony, each with a ram's horn. Look behind
them — some men bearing a box of some sort and all of
them in strange garb. They look like anything but soldiers.
Surely, they cannot be an army! There seems to be no discipline, no arms, no armour, no . . . that cannot be an army.
But they act strangely. See, they are taking a course
around our wall. Well, they seem to intend no harm. We
shall watch and see what is their intention." And so, they
watch Israel's men march around the city, then see them
return to their tents at a distance. It would have been
interesting to hear the discussions inside the wall that night.

Next day the same scene is enacted and the same wonder
grows inside the city. Finally, after three or four days of
this, wonder turns to ridicule, and Jericho's inhabitants
hurl their taunts and jeers from the wall against God's
people. The people of God never made any progress in
this world except at the expense of being laughed at and

belittled by the world. When we fight by faith we shall
always be reproached by the world and bear the shame of
the ignorant. This world, in its conceit, cannot see the
wisdom of God; hence it will look upon any who call us
to follow God's simple way as visionary and impractical.
All of God's heroes have borne such reproach. That is
what the modern church fears.

At last Jericho's army has grown accustomed to Israel's
march, and unconcern reigns upon the wall. Pity of the
poor and ignorant has arisen in their minds. But today
things take on a new interest. It is the sabbath of Israel,
and after circling the wall they do not return to their tents.
They circle it again. People inside the wall come to see
what is going on below. By the time Israel has gone
around the seventh time, the whole citizenry has no doubt
gathered to watch and to inquire into such extended, but
harmless, action. This is just what God has led them to
do. Now the Big Attraction comes into view — God!
Israel and her army fade out of the picture, and, having
done nothing but worship and witness and believe, they
blew their trumpets to announce the presence of God, and all
shouted their praises of Him who *had already given* the
city into the hands of Joshua. "The wall fell down flat."

With Jericho's armies disrupted and its people in chaotic
disorder, Israel's men went in and easily defeated them.
Utter destruction of men, women, children, oxen, asses,
and sheep was carried out with ease. "So the Lord was
with Joshua, and his fame was noised throughout all the
country." The Lord is with any man who will bow down
and worship God and acknowledge that God's way, though
and worship God and acknowledge that God's way, though
is better than our ways.

Now, how did Joshua accomplish this great victory?
And when? He accomplished the victory when he believed
God, and faith was the victory. The victory was not in
tearing down the walls and taking Jericho; the victory
was in believing that God would do it. This is the victory!

The flesh will fight this truth, for it dishonors the flesh
and honors God. But the things that are accomplished by
faith can never be done by the flesh. Why? Because that
which is done through faith is supernatural, and the flesh
knows nothing of such works.

This truth is lost to the modern day church, yet the Bible
is full of it. Churches don't tarry before God, asking Him
to do great things for them; they organize after the world
pattern, and, in the strength and wisdom of the flesh,
they rush out to do great things for God. Yet, ever the
command of God is, "Go, tell what great things the Lord
hath done for thee."

This is the witness that attracts men to God. Nobody
cares about what we can do; they want to know what our
God can do. And they are looking to us to see what He
is doing for us. We can never make a convicting appeal
to this lost world on what we can do for our God, but
when we go telling and showing what our God has done
for us, the world will listen. Always it is the miracle that
attracts.

This age is turning out preachers of promotion — "how-
to-do-it" preachers — whose business is to organize and
foster the Kingdom of God through the church. We have
trained them in the most intricate detail of what to do,
and how to do it. We have left them entirely ignorant
of what God has done and can do for us. We are preaching
a program of works throughout. We are trying to enlist

men in a program of doing things for God, and, by advertising what we have been able to do, we try to make a convincing appeal to the lost. Ours is a gospel of promotion instead of a gospel of revelation. We need prophets who can talk about God instead of promoters who can talk about us. We need leaders who can introduce us to a God of power and glory rather than leaders who propose to make gods of us. There is nothing that will separate the church from the world like the revelation of such a God.

And yet, the cry from our churches is ever, "make us gods!" We have lost the mystic God in the cloud, and as for the Moseses who linger up there with Him, we wot not what has become of them. Here are our earrings and our streamlined ideas. Get a graving tool and make us a church life that will give *us* something to do, and stop this boredom of waiting on God. And when we get through with this heathen business, what we have is a golden calf, just like the one Israel left in Egypt.

But it is recorded to the credit of Joshua's faith that, "By faith the walls of Jericho fell down, after they were compassed about seven days" (Heb. 11:30). Separated from the world and surrendered to God, they demonstrated their faith in what God had said. They obediently and in blind faith marched around the walls just as God had said, they blew their trumpets and shouted the praises of their God, and their God tore down the walls. Such is the wit~ of Joshua.

GIDEON

The Midianites, armed to the could devise, lay as thick as gra ready to spring with armed might pitiful army of Israel. Instead of su

of Israel with more men and arms, God asks Gideon to
send back all of his thirty-two thousand men except three
hundred. As a man of faith does, Gideon obeys. He
knows not how God will do it; he knows only that God
knows how He will do it. So, blindly trusting, he obeys.
With God the strategy is simple. The three hundred men
who are left, each with a candle in a pitcher and a trumpet,
take their stand around the hills above the sleeping Midianites. At a signal from Gideon, each man breaks his pitcher
revealing his candle light, and each man blows his trumpet.
The Midianites leap from their slumbers, see the lights
around the hills, imagine the woods are full of men, and,
in utter chaos, begin to fight any form that moves in the
darkness about them. They slay themselves, as all men
do who fight against God, and the result is complete victory for Gideon's little band of three hundred. "The sword
of the Lord and Gideon!"

There is not a military strategist in the world who would
have endorsed such foolishness. But "the foolishness of
God is wiser than men." Who gets the glory for this victory? Not Gideon! Not the army! Not Israel! Just God!
But the blessings of the victory fall on those who trust
Him, and who were able to believe that God had some tricks
up His sleeve which were better than the wisdom of the
flesh.

Oh, it takes real faith to believe a God like that! The
flesh will cling on with doubt and fear and caution, and
forbid any such reckless faith. "Fanaticism!" they will
hurl at you. But God will be saying all the time, "Only
believe!" Who but God could make fools of a big military
outfit as He did of the Midianites? Wonderfully simple!
Wonderfully foolish! Wonderfully effective!

But why didn't He let the thirty-two thousand soldiers do it? He tells us why in Judges 7:2: "The people that are with thee are too many for me to give the Midianites into their hands, lest Israel vaunt themselves against me, saying, Mine own hand hath saved me." God is going to have the glory for all He does. That is why He does everything in such a way that no one can say it was of man's ingenuity or wisdom. All God needed was a man who could believe Him.

DAVID

David, the shepherd lad who knew nothing about military life, was charged by his brothers with coming down from his occupation to see the battle between Israel and the Philistines. As he watched, Goliath came upon the grounds, big, fierce, heavily armed, skilful, and challenged dismay into the heart of every Israelite — every one except David. When David heard the challenge to his God, he could not stand and take it. Somewhere in the quiet of the fields he had stood before God and had been filled with the wonder of God's size and wisdom. He immediately offered to meet the giant.

After much insistence, big King Saul consents to let him try, but brings out the old clanking armour designed for a man head and shoulders above other men. David tries it on, finds himself imprisoned in it, refuses to wear it, and proposes to go out only in the name of the Lord.

Men of faith find it practically impossible to war against Satan in the garb of modern religious armour. Why? Because that armour is too often designed by the flesh, based on a competitive attack in worldly wisdom by the same methods and plans which the world uses. It is not different from the world, but is exactly like the world in that it magnifies and glorifies human efficiency to the exclusion of blind faith in a God who does things in an unworldly way. We are afraid to trust God; so, in order to guarantee that He will be a success and not embarrass us before the world, we must ground Him in that which the world recognizes as successful before we turn Him loose. To rely upon His methods is to run the risk of being branded as impractical and behind the times in modern methods of "church work." And, inasmuch as our appeal is to the world, we must not insult the world's intelligence by using methods or plans which are not derived from the best psychology and science of the day.

That may be useful in a warfare between "flesh and blood," but when we get into the warfare against "principalities, against powers, against the rulers of the darkness of this world, against spiritual wickedness in high places," we had better let God choose the armour.

So, David goes out in the armour of God — the *invisible* armour — clothed in the Name of the Most High God. Hear him declare his armour: "The Lord that delivered me out of the paw of the lion, and out of the paw of the bear, he will deliver me out of the hand of the Philistine." Of course, if we have never had much experience with bears and lions, we probably won't be very well equipped to fight a Philistine. But if once we get the idea that God *delivers us* instead of our *delivering Him,* we may catch a vision of a God whom we can trust with His own business, and, like Joshua, bow down and say, "What sayest thou to thy servant?"

The battle is already won before it starts. It wasn't a question of killing the giant; it was a question of believing.

Dear brother, let me tell you, if I had been in David's place, and hadn't won the battle of faith before I started out, you would have seen me starting at a rapid pace the other way. The place for God's people to win victory is on their knees. Can we come to the place where we can believe that God can handle His own affairs, create His own plans, work His own strategy, and do what He wants to do by ways and methods and power unknown to this world? We will have to tarry on our knees and look again into the Bible to get a glimpse of a God like that. If we want a revival of power, all the world's methods will not bring it, though they be conceived in the minds of some of our most prominent leaders. God alone can send it, and we must tarry there to let Him start it in us. And when He does send it, all our plans and methods will have to get out of the way like the flood tides wash away the works of men below it. Nothing we can do will bring such tides; they must come from Heaven. And we will have to make contact with the God who sits up there if we are to see them flow with refreshing revival. It will be nothing we do to bring it, if it come; it will be a miracle of God that will make a great appeal to the world, and with convicting power.

In the eyes of the army of Israel, not to speak of the Philistines, David was an utterly foolish boy who, desiring to be a hero, was tossing himself to a Philistine dog. He was too ignorant to know any better, but could not be restrained from his foolishness. Here again we get the world's opinion of those who trust in God. When you live in an unworldly faith you cannot be understood by people who live only in the flesh. Many a preacher or pastor has been crucified by a church that couldn't see what he saw,

and thought him visionary and impractical. Yes, men of
faith are visionary; for they "endure as seeing him who
is invisible." What a spectacle a man makes of himself
when he goes around saying he sees something others can't
see! Nobody can understand a man who lives with his
eyes glued on somebody they can't see. What he does, and
what he tries to get them to do, marks him as foolish in
their eyes. Jesus is the example. They nailed Him to a
cross because He saw things they couldn't see.

Well, little David knew he couldn't whip the giant, but
back yonder in the hills he had seen a God who could slay
a lion and a bear. He knew that God was big enough to
whip Goliath or anybody else. So he climbed up inside that
God and immediately he was just as big as God is. In
that position he could have whipped the whole Philistine
army as easily as he slew Goliath. So, he approaches the
giant and finds that the giant's pride has been hurt.

That is what the modern church fears, that unless it
approach the world in "conventional" method and wisdom
it will insult the world. To come in the "foolishness of
God" would make no appeal to the world. Besides, the
modern church is trying to make friends with the world,
not slay it. Modern Christianity does not seek to bring
a sense of conviction and death (repentance) to this world;
it is trying to socialize it and civilize it and improve it,
so that it will be fit company for God. And we must
therefore be very careful that that world respects our finesse
and efficiency and good taste as we seek to conquer it.
If we bring conviction and condemnation to sinners they
will curse us.

"Dare you to make out that I am a low-brow, a dog,
without dignity or class?" said the giant. And so, says

the world, "Do you make out that I am a depraved sinner,
a condemned and judged convict? You insult my dignity.
I am intelligent. If you have anything to offer it must be
of an intelligent order, or I shall consider you a back number and a radical, presuming upon my intelligence. Nothing but the most modern methods and ideas will make any
appeal to me. Start toward me with anything else, and I
will take your head off." And we are afraid to preach
condemnation to a world like that, for fear we will not
"win" it. We think it wiser to approach sin, both in self
and in the world, with a "saner" appeal than condemnation.
For who knows but that we might persuade the giant to
become one of us? And, seeing his great abilities, we might
revamp his talents and use them for our side!

Anyway, God and a sling shot were sufficient, just as
God and anything or anybody are, and the giant was up
against the INVISIBLE. He could see David, but he
couldn't see God. David said, "Thou comest to me with
a sword, and with a spear, and with a shield: but I come to
thee in the name of the Lord of hosts, the God of the
armies of Israel, whom thou has defied . . . . And all this
assembly shall know that the Lord saveth not with sword
and spear; for the battle is the Lord's, and he will give
you into our hands" (I Sam. 17:45, 47).

The battle is the Lord's! What a wonderful discovery
for this modern day, when we thought the battle was all
ours, and when we are not only rallying forces and training them to fight, but we have our highly trained experts
directing it. That is indeed wonderful! Now we can turn
the thing back over to the Lord and see what He can do
with it. Or will we?   ,

Well, from now on it is quick work. Just one vulnerable spot in the giant's head, but God takes hold of David's arm and, with godly accuracy, swings a stone at that spot. David prevailed, but "there was no sword in the hand of David." Remarkable! He had never been to a training school, but was the only one in the hosts of Israel who could meet the need that day!

If anyone else had done this, God would not have gotten the glory. The flesh will check up every conquest to itself unless it first be robbed of every source of self-sufficiency. Even here, silly women began to sing David's praises above Saul, wholly unaware of what David knew, that God did it. And here arose the typical jealousy of others that comes when God honors a man's faith above the wisdom of the world. "And Saul eyed David from that day forward."

Like any man of great faith, David felt humbled rather than exalted. If you have ever stood in the darkness, in utter despair, and have heard divine wings rustling above your head, you will not be inclined to boast, but to bow down. If God can do that *for* you, what could He do *against* you?

There was a great revival in Israel that day and a great conquest of the enemy. Why? Because Israel had fought a great battle? No! Because they had confessed their impotence, and God had honored the faith of His little saint and *had done something for them*. This is ever the time of revival. Let God start doing something for a church, blessing it with a presence it has not felt before, raising the hopes of the people, converting sinners, and watch the people start getting happy and praising the Lord. *Yes! Praising the Lord!* Because it is He that hath done this thing. Oh, if we had that again you would see our little

gods — the works of our own hands — go into hiding!
And people would crowd in to see who this Strange God is.

ELIJAH

We now come to Mt. Carmel (I Kings 18). Elijah
has charge of the weather, and there has been no rain on
the earth for about three years. Things are really bad,
and Ahab is blaming Elijah. Elijah counters by placing
the blame upon the sins of the people. How many times
God's servants have been accused of disturbing the peace
of the church, when all the while the blessings of God have
been cut off from the church because of the sins of the
people! The one problem of our Lord through all the ages
has been the matter of keeping His people separate from
the world. He can do great things for them, but their
iniquities can separate them from the blessings of God.
The worship of other gods stops the blessings of the One
God.

Elijah calls a great convocation upon Mt. Carmel, and
there the test comes. The prophets of Baal call upon their
gods, but to no avail. The contest becomes very intense.
They punish themselves in the flesh and cry aloud, but no
word comes from their gods. Then Elijah takes charge.
Notice something in particular: He does everything that
would be contrary to a natural and favorable condition
for fire upon the altar. Elijah did not prepare the altar
so it would succeed with just a little help from God. He
made it so that everybody would know that if God did
not do something for Elijah there was no possibility of
anything of natural origin helping out.

So often we are afraid God can't get over the hard
places unless we arrange a natural condition favorable to

Him, and streamline everything so that God can work without natural hindrances. In this way we rob God of the glory and chalk up the success to ourselves, seeing that we were smart enough to make God a success.

When Elijah got the stage set, God was to be the only Actor. And this all had a purpose. Elijah expresses it in his prayer (vv. 36, 37): "Elijah the prophet came near and said, Lord God of Abraham, Isaac, and of Israel, let it be known this day that thou art God in Israel, and that I am thy servant, and that I have done all these things at thy word. Hear me, O Lord, hear me, that this people may know that thou art the Lord God, and that thou hast turned their heart back again."

That this people may know that thou art God! That was the object of the whole thing. Therefore, everything was fixed to give God a full show: Elijah and Israel took the position of helplessness and left all to God to do something for them. Result? Fire fell, "and consumed the burnt-sacrifice, and the wood, and the stones, and the dust, and licked up the water that was in the trench. And when all the people saw it, they fell on their faces: and they said, The Lord, he is the God; the Lord, he is the God." And away went the gods and the prophets of Baal.

Now, that is the kind of revival we need. But it will never come till we acknowledge our helplessness and set the stage for God to do something for us, and let Him do it in His own way. Then the people around will be impressed with our God; they will never be impressed with us.

If we ever get a vision of that God again, we will bow down in awe and reverence. We will find ourselves confessing sin. In the sixth chapter of Isaiah you have the

vision of which we speak. As soon as Isaiah, no doubt
a good man and religious, saw God in His exalted state,
he too kissed the earth with humility and cried, "Woe is
me! for I am undone; because I am a man of unclean lips,
and I dwell in the midst of a people of unclean lips: for
mine eyes have seen the King, the Lord of hosts." Oh,
that we might again catch a glimpse of the God who can
make us bow down! But we have, through the eyes of
the flesh, seen God to be only as big as our minds and our
hands can make Him, and thus we assume the burden of
making Him a success in the eyes of the world.

MARY OF BETHANY

We choose Mary's witness because it gives us a picture
of such beautiful trust and understanding of God's ways.
The contrast between her and her sister Martha sets forth
these great truths in a striking manner. There has been
much careless instruction given on this story recorded in
the Gospel according to Luke 10:38-42. Often you hear
preachers of the how-to-do-it programs say, "Yes, we must
have our Marthas as well as our Marys." But what is
the Lord's comment on these sisters? "But one thing is
needful (not two): and Mary hath chosen the good part
(not the better part), which shall not be taken away from
her."

Was Mary indolent and lazy? I have heard it so said;
but her Lord did not say so. Was Martha more devoted
to her Lord than was Mary? Not according to our Lord.
What, then, is the secret here that makes our Lord commend
Mary and rebuke Martha for being so troubled about
many things?

It is a comment of our Lord on this busy religious life we are living, by which we are trying to show the Lord we are devoted to Him. It is a comment on our shallow concept of our Lord and His mission in this world. It is a comment on our poor understanding of what our Lord is here for, and on our inappropriate demonstration of our zeal — a zeal without knowledge.

Martha loved her Lord, but she had a shallow understanding of His heart. She is typical of the modern day church worker who is so busy she does not have time to get acquainted with her Lord. She is typical of that earthly zeal which spends itself in doing things for God without knowing what her Lord can do for her.

If a man is going to serve God, he must first sit at the feet of Jesus long enough to find out what God is like, and what would be appropriate to His needs. "Be still, and know that I am God" is a ball and chain to the feet of this fast traveling age. Churches must keep up with the times, must be alert to all new fads and customs. They must keep up with all progress and take shrewd advantage of every worldly device to make the Kingdom of God "click." We have forgotten that the Word of God is the only thing that does not change, and that our changing ways and customs and desires are but proofs of our worldly and temporal minds. The reason God does not have to change His Word and His ways is because they are perfect and endure all changes of time or custom. His methods are the same in every age, for they deal with man who is still the same, and his sin which is still the same, and through a Christ who is still the same.

But only the few who sit at the feet of Jesus will discover this. Mary sat there and listened and discovered that the best way to serve and honor her Lord was to let Him pour out His heart into hers. If we don't let God do something for us, God can't do anything. He has nothing to work on but us, and no one to give Himself to but us. God doesn't need anything Himself except somebody to whom He can give Himself. If we shut Him out of that privilege, He can't bless us.

Martha understood little of her Lord's heart. She tried so hard to serve her Lord, but with such an inappropriate *busy-ness* that the Lord had to rule it out. Mary put her devotion all into an act of worship, confessing that she had nothing to give Him but that He had everything to give her. Therefore, she would lay aside everything to let Him unburden His full heart to her worshipful soul.

What was the result? Mary discovered something Martha needed so much to learn, and that this whole world of church life needs to learn, and that is, "The Son of Man came not to be ministered unto, but to minister, and to give his life a ransom for many." That discovery brought her, a little later on, to break an alabaster box of ointment, precious above her other possessions, and anoint Him for His burial. She had found the secret of His mission, and in this act gave her heart to Him in appreciation. That was all Jesus wanted. He still wants to find those who can appreciate what He has done for them, and who will open their hearts in worship. To such hearts God will become great.

And how great was this Lord to Martha and Mary? Let me tell you. He was so great to Martha that she would set her house in complete order for Him; *He was so great to Mary that she would set the house completely aside for Him.*

If this church age would ever discover Jesus to be so great that we could set our house aside for Him, and quit driving ourselves into the sanitoria trying to set it in order for Him, we would find our hearts in condition to receive blessings which our well-organized house can never contain.

Martha made Jesus the God of her house; Mary made Him the God of her heart. And so many of us these days are busy building temples of wood and stone for Him, and are weighted down with the business of making our household orderly for Him, but we are too busy to let Him come into our hearts with a power unknown to this hour of religion.

Have we chosen the good part? More than that, dare we choose it? Are we not afraid of the embarrassment that would come to us all if we threw away our house gods and bowed down before a heart God? Are we not afraid of a revival that would cast away our gods? Do we not, in our praying, ask God to come and fit into the scheme of things we have set up, and, like the children of Israel under Aaron, have we not said, "These be the gods which brought us up out of Egypt?"

I was made sad recently in a meeting where plans were being laid for a great sweeping revival campaign. I have read and taught many books on "how-to-do-it" in the various phases of church life. I see now the unimportance of many of them.

In this meeting to which I refer they were discussing the work of a certain department in the evangelistic campaign. The earnest and godly leader of the conference distributed to each of us two legal-sized sheets of paper, clipped together, filled with single-spaced, typewritten questions and instructions for the leader of this department. There were questions on the qualifications and skill of the special leader who would come to the church for the meeting, on his personal appearance, his psychological approach to the situation, his ability to get along with the people; his relationship to the church's own established groups in his field, to their leader, and to other leaders in the church; whether or not these local groups should have a regular or special place in the revival meeting; whether or not the visiting leader should recognize in a special way the local leader; whether or not the regular routine of the established groups should be carried on through the meeting; what the visiting leader should eat and when, how he should conduct himself in homes and with relation to the pastor and the evangelist; and on and on with endless questions about personality, procedure, relationships, recognitions, and so forth; until it seemed to us that it would require the assistance of psychologists, psychiatrists, philosophers, the mayor, and the chief of police, besides all the experts in the fields represented in the church, to conduct a revival meeting with proper attention to all the items set forth in this paper. The author of it is a godly man and earnest in his field, but, like Martha, there is every possibility that he is "troubled about many things" where only one thing is needful. How did God ever conduct revival meetings before the experts got hold of the job? He seems to have gotten along well at Pentecost. I say I was made sad, because I felt that God's work was being blocked by the earnest, conscientious efforts of the flesh.

One day on an eastern train I was conversing with a Japanese girl who was probably in her late twenties. I soon learned that she was a student in an American Mission school, preparing to go back to Japan as a missionary. I had been talking quite freely, as is usual for me if any one will listen, and she had been resting her head on the back of the seat, watching the scenery as we hastened along. She quietly observed:

"The American people talk so much. They just seem to want to talk all the time. We Japanese like to be quiet. Religion to us is so much quiet; not a lot of talk. We like to worship quietly and think."

I smiled and said apologetically: "You are certainly right. I wish I could be more quiet, and your observation is timely and correct."

She hastened to explain: "I did not mean what you think. I have listened to your explanations with pleasure. But what I mean is — the girls at school; they just talk and talk about so many things which don't seem important. And much of their teaching is so unimportant."

I heartily agreed with her, of course, but I asked her for an example. "Well," she said, "for instance, I was taking an examination on a course I had studied in the mission school, on 'How to conduct the ......' (Here she mentioned the name of a familiar organization in modern church life), and the question was, 'Who should introduce new church members to the (organization)?' " Then she looked out the window with what seemed to be a sort of pity for people who deal in such trifles and quietly observed: "I don't see that it makes any difference who introduces new church members to the (organization)." To this I heartily agreed. Yet, so much of the books on "how-to-do-it" are loaded down with this kind of detail. Millions of pamphlets and books are printed, classes by the thousands are conducted in their detail, and the lives of our people are filled with so much expertness and finesse, that we feel like dumping Saul's armour into the ocean and going out with God and a sling shot to slay the giants. It will get on the nerves of any man who has contemplated God long enough to see that the wisdom of man is foolishness with God.

I have a deep regard for those who toil and work to make possible a great revival. I cannot credit myself with much success along this line. But, going back to the conference I mentioned above, I could not help moaning, "Lord, if you have to fit into all this before we can have a great revival, you will be so harrassed by our red tape that you will never be able to get to us with the blessing." I do not say this with disrespect for those who try to lead us. But I do believe our leaders have made our God small, even to the proportions of our own minds and abilities, and we are afraid to trust God with His own business. Hence, we make our plans and ask Him to follow.

Once I was talking with one of our leaders about a proposed great "campaign." I was objecting to some of his conclusions on plans and details. He said to me, "Man, this came out of the greatest minds of our convention." And in my own mind I answered, "Yes, that is exactly where it came from!"

If it be charged that I am advocating a "do-nothing" religion, I reply that I am advocating the only religion that does things that endure.

JESUS

The witness of our Lord to these truths needs only to be summarized. When did the people believe? When they saw a blind man open his eyes and see, a lame man get up and walk, a palsied man carry his bed home, demons cast out of a wild boy, a little girl get up from her death bed, a young man climb down from his coffin, a decomposed Lazarus come forth from the tomb. It was always the miracle — what God did — that made men believe. When they saw God on demonstration they were always impressed. It was this that made people turn, with hungry hearts, from the dried up ceremonialism of the Pharisees to a peasant body throbbing with the heart beat of God.

THE HOLY GHOST

Come now to Pentecost. Ten days of waiting and praying, to which nobody paid any attention except about one hundred and twenty humble disciples. But God came down, in the Holy Ghost, and began to act upon men. There was noise of a supernatural kind, and actions not of this world, and speach unworldly, and power which brought the whole city out. We have tried every way to get a crowd except letting God bring one. Men are not going out to see what men can do; they will come only when they can see God in action.

The disciples were filled with God, and through them God demonstrated His power and wisdom which was wholly different from the world's way. Methods? God had methods. His method here is simple enough for a church of five, and complex enough for a church of fifty thousand. It is simply this: *Have experience with God, and tell it to somebody.*

But if people don't have time to pray and get apart from the world, if they are so busy "running the church" that they can't sit at the Master's feet, naturally they can't be filled with the Spirit. So, filled with their own wisdom and ingenuity, and depending on their own plans copied and adapted from the world, they seek to ensnare sinners into something only a little better than what they are used to.

These disciples were warned that "without me ye can do nothing." So they waited for Him. When He came He didn't fit into any worldly schemes; He simply took over the bodies of the disciples and, with power of Heaven, moved them to do and say things this world never had seen. The Holy Ghost was, for once, unquenched. Result: they had a crowd, they preached, the Holy Spirit convicted and saved, and everybody was praising God, because God was the One who had done it all.

Nobody had to take census in Jerusalem. The population all turned out to hear the wonderful things of God and to see God-possessed human beings under the miracle power of God. I know this is a special day in the life of the church, but the same Holy Spirit is here now. Yet, He cannot kill giants while hampered by Saul's armour.

The thing that is noteworthy here is that the people were happy because the Lord was blessing. They were praising God and having favor with the people, because the Lord's favor upon them was evident to all. He was adding to them.

PETER AND JOHN

Now Peter and John go up to the temple to pray, and they find a lame man at the temple gate. Nobody had ever done anything for him except to give him enough alms to keep him living on as he was born. That is all this world can do for anybody. And the only people who have anything different to offer a helpless man are the people of God. "Silver and gold," such as the world has, "have I none."

Churches in this day think that if they can get a lot of money, build great buildings, and hire a lot of workers, they can do great things for God. Maybe so, but that is doubtful. In nearly every community there is a church which may be entirely short on silver and gold and beautiful buildings and great systems of work for social betterment, all of which seems to be the great emphasis of this hour, but they could be rich in the "such as I have." That is what the world is needing, and with that we are utterly stingy. What the world needs most, the power to get up and walk. is that in which we are poorest, and that which we use the least.

"In the name of Jesus Christ of Nazareth," the man leaped up and began praising God. What did Peter give him? God! "I have nothing to offer to you but God," said the apostle, but that was all he needed. Now God is on the stage, and the young man is leaping and praising Him. Here again is the way to get a crowd — let God do something for somebody. "All the people ran together unto them in the porch that is called Solomon's, greatly wondering." Such a feeling will never be produced by us with our ponderous figures and records of accomplishments. But let God do something for us, and the people will rush in to see it.

Peter was quick to sense the possibility of hero worship that might obtain, so he quickly told them that it was the "God of Abraham, and of Isaac, and of Jacob, the God of our fathers," who "hath glorified his Son Jesus." Then he shot home the condemnation that rested upon them in the crucifixion of this Jesus, and showed how God had ex-

alted the crucified One to everlasting rule. Therefore, repent, said he, as he went on with his sermon. He had a
crowd now, and it was a good time to preach. "Many
of them which heard the word believed; and the number
of the men was about five thousand."

Much opposition followed, as it always does when God
is working. There will not be much opposition to the works
of the flesh, for its religious program will be so much like
the world that it will be either accepted or ignored. But
let God go to performing miracles in the hearts of men, and
Satan will oppose that at once and vigorously. The *Acts
of the Apostles* is full of this record. When God works
the people are attracted, and when miracles are performed
believers are added.

Let it be once and for all understood: God must be on
display before this idolatrous world will ever be shaken
from its gods and turned to the living God. And it will
be God working *in* us and *through* us, rather than we working *for* Him, that will make manifest the miracle power
which attracts lost men to Him.

That is the purpose of miracle, from the first to the
last, to show people what God can do for us. The greatest
miracle God ever performed is the one wrought by the
Holy Ghost in us, which transforms us from sinners and
worldlings into obedient slaves of God, and which makes
us so different from the world that we will be looked upon
as not belonging here but to the family of God in heaven.
To have people walking around in the world, in whom the
power of God is manifest, is the only thing that will attract
lost men to Him. The Bible is a record of man's helplessness and God's miracle in his behalf.

If we do not come back to the miracle God, we have no hope. I wonder what would happen if our churches threw down everything for the time, at least, and, empty-handed, gathered around God in prayer and confession of sin, and said, "Lord, we cast down our idols, separate ourselves from the world, and come to thee for help. Do something for us in thine own way, and show us how to walk." A sincere attitude like that would break the flood gates of Heaven open, I doubt not, and blessing would flow in this old sinful world. That is the way it has always been. As long as we cling to our own self-sufficiency and ask God to approve it, we shall always remain helpless. Why don't we confess it and repent?

I believe the answer is in the pride of our own works. We are embarrassed to confess that we have made a mistake: that we have built a machine religion which, according to all "intelligent calculations," should succeed by virtue of its psychological fitness to the mind and natural disposition of man. We have no place in it for the miracle. Instead of pouring water all over the altar and around it, to make it unmistakable that God alone sent down the fire, we have tried to make the altar sizzle a little ourselves so that it would be easy for God to get off to a good start. And, I fear we shall never have the grace to say, "We have been wrong." May God help us!

CHAPTER III

Walled Cities: The Believer's Sins

NOW WE COME to consider the faith principle and the miracle power of God in dealing with the believer's personal life. In the preceding chapter we have seen "the Lord's doings, and it is marvelous in our eyes." Can this God help us to take the walled cities in our individual lives? Our answer is a positive yes!

The walled cities of our personal lives, occupied and fortified by the enemy, may be grouped in three realms: (1) *Our sins.* How shall we deal with sin after we are saved? (2) *Our trials and sorrows.* How can we solve life's problems and bear life's sorrows? (3) *Our witness.* How can we make ourselves become effective witnesses for Christ?

First, we shall take up the sin question.

Every believer is troubled with sins that persist in his life. He finds himself harrassed and plagued by the failures he makes in overcoming them. The Holy Spirit in the heart of every believer hates sin, but the flesh loves sin. So, the two are in conflict all the time. How shall we overcome, especially, besetting sins? The answer will require patience, but we shall be as brief as possible. Jesus said, "Ye shall know the truth, and the truth shall make you free." Now, in most problems, if we can look through them as with an X-ray and discover the truth about them, we can thereby cut the ties that bind us. Christ has already made us free; the bondage is in our failure to discover our freedom. Satan's business is to keep us in the dark, confuse us and accuse us, so that we will be discouraged. Jesus wants us to discover the truth about what He has done for us.

Let us begin with the believer's first experience. He has been saved and is happy and free. He is forgiven and cleansed, and he is in blessed fellowship with God. He feels that he will never want to sin again.

However, that good feeling dies down, and the believer is faced with the reality of fleshly desires again. Old habits and old associates come back for fellowship. In a moment of weakness, like a babe trying to learn to walk, he falls into sin. He is disappointed. He was sure he would never do this again, but he has, and he is ashamed. He hates his sin, but what can he do? After the first shock of failure is over, he hears some one saying, "Resolve now that you will never let this happen again. You must be good if you are going to be a Christian. You must do better than you did when you were lost. Admit your sin, but resolve that you will never do it again."

What Christian has not felt this way again and again, and has not heard that voice saying those very things? But that advice does not come from God; it comes from Satan. It may sound, to the untaught, like the voice of God, but it is the voice of Satan. The fleshly mind has no better understanding of God than this, so it expects this kind of advice from Him. But God has other advice.

So, with a firm resolve, the babe in Christ gets up to walk again. Maybe he holds out a little longer this time, but just the same that sin or another comes back, and suddenly he finds himself failing again. He has sinned in spite of resolve. When this happens a few times, maybe not more than two or three, Satan begins to whisper, "Well, you're not getting along very well, are you? Maybe, after all, you did not get the real thing. You have lost some of the good feeling you had, and you can't seem to walk without sin, so, if I were you I wouldn't go to church today. You will be embarrassed down there among God's children, especially since they know what you have done. Besides, it isn't necessary to be there every time the church door opens. You don't want to become radical in your religion. You might go visit your mother, or sister, or a friend today, and take a little rest from this ordeal. They don't know about your sins, and you will feel more comfortable with them. Just rest on the struggle a little, and then you can try it again after things blow over."

A discouraged believer can easily yield to this advice. Satan's first step is to get the believer embarrassed so that he will miss the church service and thus fail to hear how he might overcome his sin. After a break or two like this, and failing to be encouraged by a message from God, the believer may find himself cold and in a state of mind which can easily conclude, with Satan's help, "Well, I meant well, but I reckon I just didn't have the real thing." This will be especially true if, like the author, he was taught by older church members that he must begin being better, now that he is saved. It is almost a universal teaching in gospel churches that when we are saved we must now begin to *do better*. We shall see that this is wrong.

Another trick of Satan is to lead the believer to the other extreme. If the believer insists in struggling on and still finds his sins embarrassing, he will seek some way to

overcome. Then the devil will lead him to hear a doctrine
of sinless perfection. He will begin to investigate this doctrine and see the testimony of people every where who say
they have been sanctified, had the "baptism of the Holy
Ghost," and have come to that place where sin has been
eradicated, and they are now living above sin. With this
bright prospect in view, it is easy for the believer to "go
in deep" and get this super-spiritual "experience."

If we are seeking a second work of grace, or sanctification
on the holiness basis, or the baptism of the Holy Ghost,
Satan will help us find some sort of experience, emotional
at least, which we can identify as that which we are seeking. Remember, his business is to deceive, and especially
in religious experience. Honest, conscientious souls are his
most susceptible victims. They are the ones who have to
be on guard against the "wiles of the devil."

So, in the main, we are confronted by two wrong methods
of dealing with sin: (1) to struggle and resolve to overcome our sins, and (2) to seek a state of holiness in which
we can live above sin. Both of these fail in human life.

Of course, we are aware of the fact that there are strong
supporters of both doctrines. There are those who believe
that we can overcome sin by just resolving not to do it.
Then there are those who testify that they have been sanctified, and that this experience took away the nature and
desire of sin. Some go farther and say they have had
the baptism of the Holy Ghost, in which experience the
power of miracle has come upon them.

The Bible does not teach that anyone can achieve an
experience which eradicates all sin. I can show that the
teaching of the Bible is this: *The holier we become the more
sin we will see in our lives.* And that is why John says:

"If we walk in the light, as he is in the light, we have fellow-ship one with another, and the blood of his Son Jesus Christ cleanseth us from all sin" (I John 1:7). Now, if ever a believer could get in a state where he would not sin, it must be when he is walking in the light and having fellowship with other believers. That is the most sublime walk possible to a believer here on earth. Then, if that be true, why does the blood of Jesus have to be cleansing him from sin? The tense is present, continued action — "keeps on cleansing." It is because the believer is in the light, sees his sins, confesses them, and the blood keeps cleansing.

The examples of the Bible prove my case. One day a preacher of another denomination came in, as he said, to "have fellowship" with me. I welcomed him, and we were soon discussing Bible truth. He believed in "fall-ing from grace," as it is commonly called, so it wasn't long until we came to that parting of the ways. In our discussion on that point, I said: "Do you believe you will ever fall and be lost?" He said, "Oh, no! I am sure I never will." I asked, "Why are you so sure? If it be possible, then might not you as well as some other?" He replied ardently: "Well, the reason I never will is because I love my Lord so much I could never be disloyal to Him. Why, He is everything to me, more than my wife, my chil-dren, my business (he was a business man also), my home, — in fact, I know of nothing that could claim me away from my Lord." He grew more tender and ardent as he continued, "My Lord has done so much for me! I love Him so tenderly, I would rather give up my own life than to be disloyal to Him for one moment."

I paused a moment, then said: "You know, Brother ...., you talk like some fellows I read about in the Bible." His face grew radiant. "You remind me of a certain apostle, who drew out a sword and tried to cut a man's head off to protect his Lord. I believe he said, 'No, Lord, I'll never let you down. I will lay down my life for you any time.' But it seems to me he was making the air blue with profanity a little later on, right in the shadow of the cross, to convince people of his claim that he had never been with Jesus. Then, you remind me of another fellow in the Bible. His good-for-nothing brother, who had been gone a long time, had come home, and they were all rejoicing over his return. But that fellow wouldn't go in and join them. When his father came out to urge him to join in the rejoicing, he began to upbraid his father, and then proceeded to tell that father what a good boy he himself had been — what he had done, and what he had not done. He was a typical Pharisee who obeyed the law but didn't love nor understand sinners. He was blind to his own sin."

By this time the light was dawning on the face of my preacher friend, but I didn't let him loose. I told him of the rich young ruler and his claims for righteousness. Then I said, "There is another fellow in the Bible of whom you remind me. He was praying over in the temple one day and he said (as 'he prayed with himself'), 'God, I thank thee that I am not as other men are, extortioners, unjust, adulterers, or even as this publican. I fast twice a week, I give tithes of all I possess.' But there was another fellow over there who did nothing but confess his sin, and Jesus said he was the one who went down to his house justified rather than the other. It was the woman taken in adultery whom Jesus forgave, rather than her accusers. It was the centurion whom the Jews had recommended as worthy so that Jesus could heal his servant, who came telling Jesus that he was unworthy."

I paused for effect, as my brother's face reddened. "You know," I said, "I believe you are wrong. The Bible seems to teach that holiness consists in seeing our sins, and those of us who get close enough to God to be in the light can do nothing but confess ourselves sinners. Going back over what I have said, the holiness of the prodigal son lay in his sense of sinfulness, and the sin of the boy at home lay in his sense of righteousness. The same is true with the Pharisee and the publican. It looks to me like you are on the wrong side. As for myself, I am likely to fail my Lord at any time, and if He does not keep His blessed hand upon me, I am sure to fail. My sin, my failure, and my unprofitable service is ever before me, and I cannot find one perfect sentiment of love and devotion in my soul. And I believe that sense of my depravity and ungodliness is my holiness which God accepts."

Well, it is unnecessary to say that our conversation did not last much longer, due to lack of interest on the part of one of us. With all the cases in the Bible to the contrary, how can any one come to that boastful, self-righteous position where they say they are now free from all sin? Plainly, it is either ignorance or Pharisaical conceit. The Bible does not teach it.

Sanctification is that journey through experience which is indicated from the Red Sea onward. Some of it is educational, some disciplinary, some of it victorious living; but all for the purpose of separating God's people unto Himself and bringing expression in them of the character of God. It is no more a sudden and complete experience than does a child, which possesses the nature of its parents,

become suddenly like them in its manifest character. There
are resemblances all along the way, but maturity brings
out more of the harmony of life and disposition. Sanctification means a *holy setting apart unto God;* but it will
never be complete until this old flesh of ours has gone
through death and resurrection, at which time we shall
be ready for His full companionship and full fellowship.
Then, and only then, shall we be like Him. Does not the
Bible say so? Then, and only then, shall we be completely
sanctified. Even when Israel dwelt in the land, may I remind
you, they did not finally drive out all the enemy, but there
were left those tribes to plague and harrass them every
time they went into idolatry and began to lean upon the arm
of flesh. And the flesh in us, which has always been unregenerate and will always be until raised anew, is the ground
where Satan still has access to us, to plague and harrass
us every time we turn to other gods and lean upon the arm
of flesh. So, sanctification will continue until the "redemption of the body" through death and resurrection.

It is not my purpose here to prove these things but to
teach them. To me they are self-evident, both in the Scriptures and in experience.

One of the most apparently spiritual evangelists I ever
knew told me one time that he had experienced three works
of grace: (1) *Regeneration,* in which the new nature came
into him. This is what we commonly called "being saved."
(2) *Sanctification,* in which experience the new nature
gained the power over the old nature. (3) The *baptism of
the Holy Ghost,* in which experience the old nature was
entirely eradicated, and he was clothed with complete holiness.

Now, one can argue a doctrine, but when a man who proves his spiritual worth made a statement of experience such as that, I was up against a difficult problem. He and I found great fellowship in the Spirit, and I could not gainsay his testimony. There are many advocates of this "holiness" experience. For years I asked God to give me all the experience He had for me, but I never sought these experiences as separate works of grace. I still want all God has for me, but I am not setting up names for the experiences.

Now, I sought earnestly the answer to this matter. During this period I was standing in a revival service during the invitation, preceding which a man of ordinary preaching ability had stormed the walls vocally, emotionally, athletically and otherwise. As they gave the invitation, I turned to a slender young man at my side and asked, "Have you been saved?" He emphatically replied, "Yes, sir! Saved, sanctified, and got the baptism of the Holy Ghost." I learned he had been at the "altar" during the preceding services and had come up with the "experiences" he professed. Knowing his capacity for understanding these doctrines, I was made to doubt. But I did see one possibility: If you have been taught that something is possible in experience, your doctrine may lead you to seek it. After all, doctrine is like a railroad track, it directs the train. And what we have been taught in the Scriptures, that is, whatever interpretation we have of them, may lead us to seek the experience which we have been taught is possible.

I do not believe that this young man had the ability to judge whether or not the Scriptures teach all these experiences; hence, I think he had been seeking what others had taught him, and, having found some "experience" which he thought answered to that which he was seeking, he accepted that as the answer. Such seekers are often urged by others to confess what they "feel."*

During my period of spiritual research on this matter, I received a letter from a woman in the south. She had read an article of mine on "The Baptism of the Holy Ghost," in which I had said that there is no such thing for the individual. She wrote me emphatically: "You are just twenty-seven years too late to tell me that there is no such thing as the 'Baptism of the Holy Ghost' for the individual believer." Then she went on to tell me in detail how twenty-seven years ago God came upon her in this "experience" and that there raged in her body an actual fire for many hours, during which all sin was burned out, and so on. It was quite an experience. I must confess I never had such and am not qualified to judge what she had. We find many people who give testimony of such experiences, varying, of course, with the individual.

From these we could go on into what is often termed "holy rollerism," with its varying "experiences" known in the flesh, and come to the extremes of "snake handling" and "cult killings" for sacrifice, and many other types of emotional extremes.

I have not come to these conclusions quickly. I have studied the Word prayerfully, and with deep desire to know the experiences which God has for His children. I have looked upon all claims of "holiness" without prejudice, to face whatever truth there may be in them. But my study of the Word, my observation of others over long periods, my discussions with others who claim a sort of "holiness"

---

* In my tract on "Saved or Deceived, Which?" I show the two kinds of *conviction, repentance,* and *conversion,* possible in "experience."

experience, and an honest analysis of myself, have brought me to the final conclusion which I here express in two parts: (1) I believe we shall never be without the carnal nature until death, and (2) "the carnal mind is not subject to the law of God, neither indeed can be." I also believe that as we come into more light, that is, more fellowship and communion with God, we will see more and more of our sins and increase in the hatred of them. In this way God and the believer are in complete harmony, and, in such a walk, "the blood of Jesus Christ His Son keeps on cleansing us from all sin." This is walking in the light. In such a walk, with such communion, and with such an attitude on the part of the believer toward sin, the Spirit wins over the flesh and renders it ineffective.

But what about the breaking of that fellowship? Unconfessed sin is all that can break it. When the believer breaks that Spirit-walk with God, that is, when he yields Satan access to the flesh and is tempted to consort with the world, he will find himself plagued by the heathen tribes which become God's instruments of discipline, and sin will turn out according to its inevitable end. God's child will always be sick of the results and thus be brought to confession. The flesh is the only ground where Satan has access to the believer. As long as we abide in the Spirit we are secure from his attacks and will not fulfil the lusts of the flesh (Gal. 5:16). If we neglect that walk we are subject immediately to his approach.

And what is it to abide in the Spirit? To have no known sin unjudged or unconfessed; to have Him in everything in our lives; to be willing to have Him reign over us; and to go to Him with all our problems and trials. In other words, a completely open life with God, standing in judgment before Him at all times.

But someone may ask, "What about the baptism of the Holy Ghost? Does not that deal with the sin problem?"

I cannot take space to go into that here, at least to any adequate extent, but I am quite sure of the ground I take. There is no such thing as the baptism of the Holy Ghost for the individual believer. Many have had "experiences" which they have called by this designation, but these have varied with the individual. It is easy to misinterpret "experience" if we do not stick closely to the Word.

The "baptism of the Holy Spirit" is accepted categorically as a biblical doctrine, but the Bible does not use such a designation. John the Baptist prophesied that Jesus would baptize the disciples in the Holy Ghost, and on the day of Pentecost that baptism took place. But that was a baptism of the *body* of Christ — the church — and not of individuals. And its purpose was not to purify or make better those who shared in the baptism, but it was to accredit the church, to identify it as God's body here on earth, and to dedicate it for His indwelling.

There is a sense in which every believer is baptized into the death and resurrection of Christ. This is identical with what we call regeneration (Rom. 6:3, 4). The type of this experience is the Red Sea. But the type of the baptism at Pentecost is the Shekinah glory which came upon the tabernacle, dedicating and accepting it as the dwelling place of God on earth. That sign appeared in the tabernacle, and in the temple, and in the temple rebuilt, but it was always a sign that God had accepted these buildings as His dwelling place on earth for those respective times.

The whole idea is the *incarnation.* The tabernacle fore-shadowed the day when God would come to dwell in our flesh. By the Shekinah glory He took up His abode in the tabernacle and the temples. Then came Jesus, God in the flesh. In Jordan the Holy Spirit, foreshadowed in the Shekinah glory, came down upon the body of Jesus, and the voice of the Father identified Him as His Son and the earthly body of God among us. When Jesus went away He left another body of flesh here — the church. On the day of Pentecost, the Spirit descended upon that church to dedicate and identify it as His dwelling place here in the earth and as the body through which He would speak to the world. It was thus empowered with miraculous gifts.

It is true that there were subsequent baptisms following Pentecost, but their purpose was to identify the church as the body of Christ in the world. To see why there must be this sign of the supernatural upon the church, and to see why there must be a convincing demonstration of power and glory, one must look at the background. The Jews had no idea of God having anything to do with other nations. They expected God to continue to express His will and purpose through them. It took some very convincing proof to break down the middle wall of partition and get the Jewish brethren to see that God was to bring all nations into His body. Thus it was necessary to let this baptism come upon enough of the different groups to convince them of God's purpose.

The argument is very clear on this point.

When Philip went down into Samaria, many people were saved. The Samaritans were, of course, a mixed race, and the Jews looked upon them with scorn. God demonstrated, by this baptism, His purpose to save and incorporate them, as well as the Jews, into His body, the church. In Acts 10 we find the account of Peter and Cornelius, and the visions which led them together in God's purpose to save the Gentiles. As Peter preached at the house of Cornelius the Holy Ghost *fell* on all them that heard the Word. And why were they astonished? "Because that on the Gentiles also was poured out the gift of the Holy Ghost" (v. 45). We know that this is a fulfilment of John Baptist's prophecy, for Peter tells us so in Acts 11:15-16, and identifies this spiritual demonstration with the first one at Pentecost. To prove that it was a *sign,* rather than an individual experience, Peter says, "Forasmuch as God gave them the like gift (what gift? The Holy Spirit!) as he did unto us, who was I, that I could withstand God?" (v. 17). The meaning is further affirmed in the next verse: "When they heard these things, they held their peace, and glorified God, saying, Then hath God also to the Gentiles granted repentance unto life." Why did they not say, "granted the baptism of the Holy Ghost?" Because the baptism was a *sign* that, to the Gentiles also — and the word *also* is very significant — God hath granted *repentance unto life."* That is, plainly, God is going to save the Gentiles *also* and bring them into the one body.

These spectacular demonstrations of power, commonly called the baptism of the Holy Ghost, enabling certain groups to speak in tongues and perform miracles, are manifestly to identify the ONE BODY of Christ in this world, and to break down all Jewish ideas that this one body is restricted to Jews only.

Now, Apollos had been preaching at Ephesus, no doubt, and was now at Corinth. The account is in Acts 19. Paul came to Ephesus and found certain disciples, about twelve, there, who seemed not to know anything about the Gospel other than what John had preached. Here again the demonstration was repeated to acquaint them with the fact that the Holy Ghost had made His entrance into the body, and that this body was to include all peoples. So, Paul informs them and brings them up to date, and there, by the laying on of hands (which was apostolic and not general), the Holy Ghost was given to them. Thus, representative groups had had this supernatural blessing, so that no one could say that the church was restricted to any particular nationality or people. Jews, Gentiles, Samaritans, and maybe one or two other groups, were blessed with this *sign* — the blessed Shekinah glory — identifying them all as a part of the *one body*.

If this had been an individual blessing, and not a sign, certainly it missed many others who were saved. Paul himself was not "baptized" but filled with the Spirit. In order to be brief, we refer the reader to Acts 5:14; 2:47; 13:47-48; the first convert in Europe, Lydia; the Philippian jailer and his household; believers at Mars Hill; and many others who were saved, but had no "baptism." All received the Spirit, and some were, like Paul, filled with the Spirit, but there was no baptism.

Clearly, this "baptism" is an identifying sign from God upon various groups, so that all may know that this *one body* — the fleshly body of the Lord in the world today — is to be composed of all nations, and that it is to be the one place in which God will dwell in the earth and through which He will do His work.

Notice that each reference to this baptism, for instance, Peter's apology on the Gentile matter in Acts 11:16ff, brings out the idea of the one body composed of both

Jew and Gentile. This is further noted in such references
as Eph. 2:14ff: "For he is our peace, who hath made both
one, and hath broken down the middle wall of partition
between us; having abolished in his flesh the enmity, even
the law of commandments contained in ordinances; for to
make in himself of *twain one new man,* so making peace;
and that he might reconcile *both unto God in one body* by
the cross: and came and preached peace to you which were
afar off (Gentiles), and to them that were nigh (Jews).
For through him we *both* have access by *one Spirit* unto the
Father" (Author's italics). The verses that follow continue
the explanation of the *one body* made out of both Jew and
Gentile, and this body is "for an habitation of God through
the Spirit," just as the tabernacle and temple were for His
habitation in the things that represented Christ in them.
And that acceptance of God of those buildings in the Old
Testament was attested by the Shekinah glory, symbol of
the Spirit, just as this new temple, the church, was dedicated
and accepted and identified as God's dwelling place by the
baptism of the Spirit upon it.

That identification having been established here in the
world, the indwelling of the Spirit in believers, "who are
builded together (in Him) for an habitation of God through
the Spirit," is a permanent fact for this age. Thus, all
believers are born of the Spirit, or, baptized by the Spirit
into the death and resurrection of Christ (Rom. 6:4), which
is the same as being born of the Spirit, and are permanently
indwelt by the Spirit, as well as often filled by Him, until
death. But nobody, since those special times of the identification of the *one body* — the church — as God's temple
here in the world, has had a personal, individual "baptism
of the Holy Ghost."

I doubt not that many, taught to seek this baptism, have earnestly and conscientiously done so and, likely, have been filled with the Spirit. This "experience" they have identified as the "baptism" they were seeking and have been satisfied that what they sought they had received.

I am quite sure that the same is true of so-called "sanctification" or "second work of grace." Those who have been taught to seek this "experience," and are looking for something which will fit the description, have earnestly yielded themselves to God and found a filling of the Spirit which they identified as what they were seeking. The first filling of the Spirit may bring great joy and release which they have hitherto not known, and it would be easy to identify this as "sanctification," "second work of grace," or "the baptism of the Holy Ghost," depending on what is being sought. And there is that other possibility, which, from observation, is quite probable, that Satan actualizes the doctrine which these errorists believe and gives a satisfying "experience" with zealous demonstrations which they have deducted from Scripture. For certainly, all that we see of so-called spiritual phenomena is not just of the flesh, that is, hysteria; but there must be some connection with a "spirit" which can deceive the seeker with an "experience" that resembles these first demonstrations of the Holy Ghost as recorded in the Bible.

These "experiences" invariably bring claims of holiness. But, as we have said, a deeper life with God makes one more painfully conscious of sin, and drives one constantly to Christ in confession, whereupon he constantly receives forgiveness and cleansing. The consciousness of holiness and freedom from sin is not in keeping with Bible examples which we have given. Sanctification, therefore, must be a process of growth in Christ-likeness, which has the effect of making us more conscious of our own sin, more conscious of His righteousness and of the fact that our hope lies in His judgment on the Cross for us. This exalts Christ and humbles us; the other position exalts us and blinds us to our sin. After all, did not the Holy Spirit come to convict of sin, of righteousness, and of judgment?

The unregenerate man, without any provocation on the part of the Holy Spirit or the gospel, is, in a sense, unconscious of his sins. True, in a moral sense he is conscious of his misdeeds and is mentally aware of his course, but as to their larger moral and spiritual involvement he is unconscious of his sins. If you challenge his life, he will immediately begin to make out a case for himself and build up for himself quite a good character.

When the Gospel is preached and the Holy Spirit works upon him, he is brought into what we commonly call a state of conviction. This is nothing less than a spiritual awareness of sin and its consequences. A fear of meeting God on this sinful basis comes into his heart, and he becomes concerned. He has come into court, the witness of the gospel and the Spirit have testified against him, and he feels a sense of conviction before God.

If he proceeds to repentance, which is a willing acceptance of the court's judgment and a plea of guilty, and to faith in the death of Christ as the answer to his sins, he is saved. The Holy Spirit is now within, to dwell and abide there. The Holy Spirit has much to do, but one of His chief works is to make and keep us conscious of sin. Only God is sensitive to the presence of sin. If God did not dwell in the heart we would still be like the unregenerate, unconscious of our sins. But God in the Holy Spirit is now within, and He is sensitive to the presence of sin.

The Holy Spirit provokes in us a desire to be holy, for He is holy. Then, by this very contrast of desires provoked in us and the desires which arise from the flesh, we are made to see how utterly hopeless is the battle against sin; that we never can, in the flesh, be anything but what we are. It is thus that we are driven to look to Christ for help, and thus we yield to the Spirit's leading. This attitude of yielded dependence on the Spirit enables Him to have full possession, and He can work in us the fruit of the Spirit. But the more the fruit of the Spirit becomes manifest in us and to us, the more despicable and hated will the works of the flesh become, so that we shall thus proceed to a better state of conduct outwardly. It is the growth of life within, filling us with godly fruitage, that possesses the life and causes the works of the flesh to cease their expression. But though the works of the flesh decline in their expression, the quality of the flesh ever remains the same, and the moment we cease to walk in the Spirit we shall begin to fulfil the desires of the flesh. The flesh is Satan's only ground on which he may approach us, and he watches ever for that breach of fellowship in the Spirit which renders him his opportunity to make us fail.

There will be more on this subject later.

CHAPTER IV

Walled Cities: The Sin Question (Continued)

IN THE preceding chapter we have seen that the sin question cannot be dealt with (1) by resolution against it, nor (2) by the other extreme, namely, spiritual experiences in which the sinful nature is eradicated. What, then, is the remedy for sin in the life of the believer?

The answer lies in a God who is able and willing to handle the sin question for us, just as He handled the salvation question for us. For us, the answer is faith. It is not a question of getting God to do something for us that He has not already done; it is a question of entering, *by faith,* into what has already been done. When we know the truth, we will find that the question of sin in our lives has been dealt with, just as it was when we were saved.

God has never asked a poor sinner to do anything about his sins except to confess them. He does ask him to believe and accept what God has done about them. As we progress in faith we have the victory.

Let us go back to the experience of salvation. We struggled with our sins but found ourselves helpless to do anything about them. When we finally came to the conclusion that we were helpless and hopeless, and that we could never do anything that would satisfy God about our sins, we were led by the Spirit to trust in Jesus the Saviour, only to find that He had done all that God required for our sins. We were bought and redeemed by the price of His blood, and God was satisfied. That was true all the time, but we found it only when we believed it. Then we felt the freedom which faith brings. We were born of a new understanding, which became our realization of eternal life, and joy was the result.

Now faith will also bring us to see that Jesus has done all that is necessary about our sins after we are saved, just as He had when we were saved.

When God gave His Son for us, that covered the entire sin question. When we, by faith, received that Son, He became, to us, all that we ever need for time and eternity. We can illustrate this by a story, which, I am told, is true. I may not have the accurate details, but, in the main, it is true.

Once there was a rich young man who called on a preacher to perform a wedding ceremony for him. Like most preachers, this one was limited in this world's goods, and so, he and his wife looked upon the wedding fee as being possibly more than the ordinary fee. The wedding was an extravagant one, and gifts from the groom were in keeping with the event. All the principals in the wedding shared in rather extravagant favors. The preacher received, as his favor, a pair of kid gloves. This, he thought, was quite out of keeping with the rest of the event, but preachers learn to take things as they come, and he went home and presented the gift to his wife. With his explanation of the matter there came some disappointment to her, as it had to him, but healing their disappointment with a few half-jovial remarks, he tossed the gloves into a drawer.

Several months later he dressed up to go upon a journey to a convention in a distant city. As his wife brushed him off and tidied his clothes, she looked him over and said, "Dear, you look mighty nice; why don't you wear those gloves? After all, they are nice gloves." He agreed and immediately opened the drawer and took out the gloves. As he pressed his hand into one of them, he found the fingers blocked. Turning one of the fingers of the glove inside out, he found in it a ten-dollar bill. Immediately his wife "took over," and soon they had found a ten-dollar bill in each of the ten fingers.

Now, this story illustrates the truth we have stated. When the gentleman gave this preacher the gloves, he gave him all that was in the gloves, but months had passed before they had appropriated *what was already theirs*. And when God gave His Son for us, then to us, He gave all that Jesus can ever mean to a sinner in time and eternity. Perhaps it will take us all of time and eternity to know the fulness of what God has given us. Yet, it is all ours now!

So, there is a remedy for sin in the life of the believer, and that remedy is the same Jesus who saved us.

This is wonderfully set forth in the *Letter to the Romans*. Paul discovers four laws, which he sets forth in this letter, and his progression in experience covers exactly the experience of Israel from Egypt to Canaan.

First, he finds that "all have sinned, and come short of the glory of God." In terrible description Paul sets forth the sinfulness of man, and the awful state of sin into which he has sunk. Thus, he concludes, in 3:23, that we have all shared in the awful fate. Unless help from some other source besides man come to us, there is not the slightest hope for either Jew or Gentile.

Second, he discovers that we are "justified freely by his grace through the redemption that is in Christ Jesus"

(3:24). "Therefore being justified by faith, we have peace with God through our Lord Jesus Christ" (5:1). *Justified* is a legal term and has to do with court action. It does not mean that a man is any holier after he is justified than he was before, so far as he himself is concerned. It simply means that, *in the eyes of the law,* he is blameless. To justify a criminal does not mean to make him any less a criminal in experience, but to make him without offence in the eyes of the law. This requires some one else to take his place.

Jesus was the Holy One; we are the sinners. Yet, in the eyes of the law of God, Jesus becomes the sinner and we become the Holy One. It is not true in our experience that we are holy, any more than it is true in Jesus' experience that He is unholy. But in the eyes of the law we have exchanged places. On this our hope must rest, for there "is no other name" in which we can find this justification.

Now let us bring the comparison up to this point. The plight of the sinner, which Paul first discovered, corresponds to the bondage of Egypt. God has to send help to release a sinner. The sacrifice of the lamb, of course, is a type of Christ's death for the sinner, and that which protects us from the "death angel," but the Red Sea is a type of the experience worked in the believer, wherein the Holy Spirit baptizes him into the death and resurrection of Christ. This is regeneration in its complete experience of repentance, faith, and new life through the Holy Ghost in us. I have no desire here to try to analyze it in its sequences as to time or operation. It all comes in one great saving experience, but there are always two realms of its operation: One is that which is done on God's book *for* us, and the other is the spiritual realization of our hope *in* us.

Suffice it to say that Paul found that a sinner could, by the law of the Sacrifice and faith, be justified and know it. In this the sinner found that God had been reconciled to him by Christ, and that he could be reconciled to God by faith in that Christ.

Now the third law that Paul discovered was that what he wanted to do in the Spirit he was hindered from doing by the flesh. "I find then a law, that when I would do good, evil is present with me," and, "the good that I would, I do not: but the evil which I would not, that do I" (Rom. 7:21, 19).

The word "law" as used here does not mean something that the legislature has passed. It means a principle of control in the life. When Isaac Newton was lying under an apple tree, and an apple fell and hit him, he began to inquire what made the apple do that. He discovered a "law" of gravitation: any object heavier than air, when loosed from its moorings above, will fall toward the center of the earth. And, this is not just an occasional happening; it happens every time. So, Paul found that every time he would do good evil was present to hinder him. It was a law that bound him. The flesh had him tied so that the Spirit could not operate freely within him.

As William Newell says in his *Romans Verse by Verse,* Paul cried out for a *deliverer.* He had a Saviour, but now he wanted a deliverer who could release him from the sin that bound him in experience.

My good friend, Dr. Ralph A. Herring of Winston-Salem, N.C., has supplied me with an excellent illustration for this thought. Here is an airplane sitting on the runway. It is pinned to the ground by the law of gravitation. Gasoline, a potential power, is brought from a source wholly apart from the plane. It is not a part of the plane. It is poured into the plane and then ignited by the proper devices. That power drives the plane out against the air, and, by sheer power of the gasoline, the plane is lifted in victory over the law of gravitation. As long as that power is applied, and the plane abides in that power, it continues to overcome. When the power is cut off, the plane is drawn down by the law of gravitation.

Paul cried out for a deliverer. He found the same Jesus who had saved him to be his Deliverer. Through the Holy Spirit, poured into the heart of Paul, he found himself able to overcome the other law in his members. This was the fourth law he discovered. "For the law of the Spirit of life in Christ Jesus hath made me free from the law of sin and death" (Rom. 8:2). That is, the Spirit in us is able to overcome the power of the flesh. This is what is meant by the present tense of the old formula of salvation: (1) We were saved from the penalty of sin. (2) We are being saved from the power of sin. (3) We shall be saved from the presence of sin.

Thus, the question now is not, "How shall I be saved from the presence of sin?" as our holiness friends insist, but, "How shall I be delivered from the power of sin?" The answer is, "the same Christ who saved us." This gives sense to all the scriptural admonitions to abide in the Spirit.

Now going back to the figure of Israel's journey from Egypt to Canaan, this period in a believer's life, where sin defeats the good he would do, is set forth in the wilderness wanderings. They have believed in a God who could take them through the Red Sea, but they are trying to find their own way now in the wilderness. They did not exercise faith in that same God to give them victory over the strong-

holds of the heathen in that land. Thus the believer fails
to trust that same Christ who saved him to give him victory
over sin. He finds himself wandering in the wilderness of
failure, with the flesh warring against the Spirit, trying to
find his own way through these perplexing and conflicting
pathways. When he comes at last to the truth, that he
cannot find the answer to the sin question in himself, he
may come then to Jordan and go over to helpless trust
in the same Christ who brought him into this life. Here
he will find that "the law of the Spirit of life in Christ
Jesus has made me free from the law of sin and death,"
and feel, at last, a sense of victory over sin.

Does this victory consist in coming into power to quit
sinning entirely? No, that is not the meaning of this victory.
It is mysterious and can be understood only by the spiritual
mind. It is a victory, first, *of absolute faith.* It will be
at first a matter of accepting things as God says they are,
entirely on faith, without seeing the evidence in experience.

Go back now to the sixth chapter of Romans, and take
a position on faith. The question is, "Shall we continue
in sin?" If not, how shall we keep from it? Remember,
God told Joshua he could take all the ground on which he
set his foot. That is, *there can be no gain until we have
first believed.*

First, in Romans 6:3, 4, Paul recounts the ground on
which we must set our feet. "Know ye not, that so many
of us as were baptized into Jesus Christ, were baptized
into his death? Therefore we are buried with him by baptism into death: that like as Christ was raised up from the
dead by the glory of the Father, even so we also should
walk in newness of life." His reasoning continues through
verse 10. In verse 7 he states the final truth for the sinner:

"For he that is dead is freed from sin." That is, he has paid the death penalty.

In this passage we find out that, as far as God is concerned, the sin question is settled. We can never make progress in outward conduct until we find the truth about the sin question as God sees it. We must come to His position, that the sin question is forever settled as far as He is concerned. This takes faith. The flesh will ever be bringing up conduct, and Satan will be constantly saying, "What about that? Look at the things you do. What are you going to do about them?" He will be constantly harrassing us about our sins, and we will, perhaps, try to curb those sins to keep from being embarrassed. It is this that he wants to provoke us to do. He desires to force us into the battle to help ourselves, for he knows we will fail if we do.

All right, what should the believer do? Do what the 11th verse of Romans 6 tells us to do — reckon it exactly the way God does. It is that way; reckon it that way. When God gets us to counting things like He counts them He can have our confidence to work in us. *Faith is the basis of all works in us.* Absolute surrender of all self-sufficiency and resourcefulness of self, and absolute faith in God to do something about our sins, is the attitude the believer must take.

First, accept God's statement that He has *already* dealt with the sin question, and that, instead of being offended at our sin, like a loving Father, He is sympathetic and wants to help us to overcome. So He calls His child who has failed and says lovingly, "Don't worry about that. I've paid for all that. Just believe that I am sympathetic and eager to help you, and have complete confidence in me that I will help you. Reckon it the way I do, and leave it to me. I am the only one who can do anything about sin, anyway, and I have already done it. Just trust it to me, and don't worry."

You see, the question is, "Can you believe?" Is not that the question that came to you when you were under conviction and you could not help yourself? Didn't you turn the whole sin question over to God and tell Him there was nothing you could do? And didn't He take hold of your problem and tell you in sweet gospel sounds that He had already settled the sin question? And when you believed that, didn't you have peace? Then what did you do in that matter? Nothing but trust. Now you are crying out for a *deliverer* — somebody who can deliver you from the power of sin, and you will find that you can do no more about this problem than you did the other. You will have to leave this also with the same Christ who gave you hope. So, you cross Jordan in absolute surrender, on the sin question, and trust God to perform, in His own way, the matter of bringing into captivity every thought to the obedience of Christ. "For though we walk in the flesh, we do not war after the flesh: (for the weapons of our warfare are not carnal, but mighty through God to the pulling down of strongholds;) casting down imaginations, and every high thing that exalteth itself against the knowledge of God, and bringing into captivity every thought to the obedience of Christ" (II Cor. 10:3-5).

Now, again we say, the flesh will hate this doctrine. It is much easier for the flesh to tackle the sin problem and believe that through restraint and self-discipline it can curb sin. Satan is happy when the believer tries to settle the sin question in this way. Self-reform after salvation is just as bad as it is before. Can we trust God to take care of our conduct as well as save our souls? Ever it is the question, "Can you believe?"

When I have preached this doctrine, people have said to me, how do you apply this in your own life? Well, here is the answer.

I have sins, like all believers. If they are not crimes, they are sins just the same. I see more sin in my life now than I ever did, and that encourages me to believe I am making progress. I am in the light more than I was. But I hate my sin more than I ever did. I find Satan is more determined to attack me now than ever. There is greater conflict now with the powers of darkness, and the attack is more subtle and in constantly varying forms. As far as I am concerned I am never secure for a moment. But as far as God is concerned, I am ever secure. Hence, I trust in Him. I know that He wants to help me. The Spirit in my heart ever prompts me to confess my sin and be perfectly honest about it.

If I do others wrong — and it is quite unknown to me that I intentionally do this — I am glad to confess my wrong to the one I have injured, as well as to God. I see nothing but the natural fruit of the Spirit in this. Any believer ought to be willing to do this. So, confession of sin to others and to God keeps me in fellowship, and thus His life can flow into me and His Spirit works His fruits in me. This should be the ordinary life of a believer who has made surrender.

But, they ask, what if a sin continues to plague and harrass you, coming back again and again? What do you do then?

I stand on my ground and say, "Lord, I hate that sin; but that is just the way I will do if you don't keep your hands on me. I can't put away sin; you will have to do it." Then I come to my ground of faith again and say, "Lord, you and I together hate this sin. I want to be delivered from it. If I fight to restrain myself in my own strength, I will simply bottle the thing up in my heart. It must be put on the cross. So, I look to you now to do something for me, and do away with that sin." In simple faith I leave it there.

His remedy varies. Sometimes He lets the sin turn out in such a way as to kill my love for it. Just makes me sick of it. Other times He fills my life with something better, and suddenly I realize I had forgotten it. When the believer keeps his heart open in confession it is easy for God to fill it with something else. Then sometimes He puts me through trial and prunes the tree. Suffice it to say, whatever He does, He is the Great Physician, and I let Him prescribe and apply His remedy, as a loving Father to His helpless child. Do you see what I mean? "I yield" to Him, and that puts me in his hands.

How do I know God will do this for me? I take it on faith. He alone can; so I trust it to Him. What do I do about my sins? I do nothing but look to Christ for help. Thus yielded, I find the law of the Spirit of Life in Christ Jesus making me free from the law of sin and death. I know this will work.

I know my reader is almost ready to turn back, feeling that this way is the lazy man's way, and too easy. He thinks it must be harder than that. But, is not that exactly what we preach to the lost sinner, trying to show him that God has done all for him that can be done, and that God is waiting for him to accept that and trust? And when you and I came to see this truth, did we not stand on the brink of faith, trembling, almost afraid it was too easy and would not work? And when we looked back to self, did we not see absolute despair? For what could we do for ourselves? It was Christ or perish! So, we cut all the strings, fell forward into His loving arms, and let Him have complete control. And what did we find? That Jesus saves! And afterward it was so clear, we wondered why we ever doubted.

But it wasn't easy to believe, was it? I remember going back to my old home community and preaching this way of salvation to the home folk. A man who had long been a moralist, even participating in religious work, listened to one of my sermons. At the close he came to me and said, somewhat in derision: "Well, where did you get this easy way of being saved?" I replied, "What easy way?" He said, "Why, this easy way of just believing and claiming the promise. Not a thing to do but just say, 'Jesus paid it all,' and that settles it. Mighty fine, if true. Didn't know it could be that easy." There was a derisive smile on his face. I said, "Do you think that is easy?" He replied, "Why if it were that easy, anybody could be saved." Then I said, "I wonder if it really is so easy. Can you believe it and accept it? Is it that easy?" He hesitated, then his face grew red. I insisted, "Just go ahead, and believe it. If you do you are saved. God's Word says so, and I would like to see you do it. Jesus died for you; do you believe it? If so, will you accept it and depend on that alone to save you?" He halted a moment, then turned away, saying, "Ay, I can't see it."

No, it is not easy. Only by the Spirit's power can we do it. It is ever the question, "Can ye believe?" All things are possible to him that believeth.

And that is the way it was with us, was it not? It all hung on that transforming moment when we trembled and dared to trust Him alone.

Now, if it be difficult to get a sinner to see that this absolute faith is that which brings him into God's blessing, is it any wonder that the believer stands on the same brink of faith and hesitates, as he wonders whether or not God can do something about his sins that plague his life? The same faith that saved us brings also the Deliverer who, through the Spirit, enables us to overcome, but only when we trust it all absolutely to Him. It is faith that enables God to work in us. When we trust, God does.

Jesus alone is ever the answer to the sin question in its penalty, in its power, and in its presence. He alone will bring us forth at last without sin. But just as the flesh wanted to help save us, it will want to help reform us, and any resort to its wisdom or strength or ingenuity will be utter failure. Here is where Satan works — in the flesh — and he wants us to bring the battle there where he can have a hand in it and thus deceive us. We must ever look to Jesus. The flesh will never be able to produce anything but its own shameful works.

CHAPTER V

Walled Cities: The Sin Question (Continued)
Forgiveness and Cleansing

BEFORE we leave the sin question we must look at the matter of forgiveness and cleansing, for there is much misunderstanding in the minds of believers on this point. Let us go to John's first letter and pick up a well-known formula of God's dealings with us on the matter of our sins.

First, John says we do sin. He admonishes us not to sin, just as the law tells us not to disobey God. But, knowing that we will sin, the Spirit, through John, tells us how to deal with it.

The first thing he tells us is not to deny that we sin; for, if we do, we deceive ourselves, and the truth is not in us (I John 1:8, 10). That settles that. Now, the next thing is to confess our sins. Notice now, he does not say to atone for sins; just confess them (verse 9). And, "If we confess our sins, he is faithful and just to forgive us our sins, and to cleanse us from all unrighteousness." John repeats for emphasis and clarity, then adds a further statement in the second chapter, first and second verses. "Sin not," he says, but, "if you do sin, remember that you have an Advocate with the Father, Jesus Christ the righteous."

Now, this is what we mean when we say that we must keep on the ground of faith. What goes on down here in our hearts depends on what goes on up there at the throne of God. The Spirit is down here in us, telling us to confess our sins. That is all we can do. But when we have done that, let us not despair; let us look up there and see what is taking place. We will at once discover that our Lawyer is up there at the throne handling our case for us, and that He Himself is the payment or sacrifice for our sins. Knowing that that is the end of sins up there, our faith transfers the blessing to our hearts, and we have peace here.

Is that too easy? Well, how else can it be done? Who else can pay for sins but Jesus? And when He died for us we were all nineteen hundred years in the future; so, He died for all the sins we have committed and all we are going to commit. When we trusted Jesus to save us, we were put in the position of one who never sins — never will sin. That is what it means to be justified. Now, we are still sinners in experience, but we are *put in the position* of Him who is holy, because He was put in our position on the cross. Thus the sin question, as to penalty, was settled forever for us. Now we are dealing with sins in our lives. They are all paid for and will never be charged against us, but they must be forgiven. And why? Now let my reader give close attention here.

Let us be sure we have the facts in mind. On God's book the believer is a dead sinner, through the death of Christ. Thus the sinner is pronounced dead. The death penalty squares every sin we have committed or will commit. You can kill a man only once, and that pays for all his crimes. So, the believer, on God's book, is a sinner who has died according to the law, and God is satisfied. He is reconciled. Thus, on God's book, the record shows that I, as a sinner, am dead, but as a believer I am alive, and both of these positions are put to my credit through Christ who died and arose for me. On this my faith rests. God does not, therefore, charge any sin against me whatever (Rom. 4:8). Yes, this is hard for the unspiritual mind to believe, but it is true. Then, if there is no sin charged against me, what is the necessity of forgiveness? What is there to forgive?

Forgiveness and cleansing have to do with the life of a child with its Father; it has nothing to do with a sinner and the law. The sinner has, by faith, died, and the law has been satisfied. God's wrath has been appeased and He is reconciled. Forgiveness and cleansing have to do with a believer in his walk and fellowship with his Father.

God never forgives a sinner until he becomes a believer. Forgiveness and cleansing are blessings that come to the believer because he is a child of God. They are not necessary to salvation; they are because of salvation. They do not bring eternal life; they are the blessings of eternal life. A sinner trusts *Christ* as Saviour — that is, he falls upon *Christ* as his only hope. His faith in Christ makes Christ his Saviour, and on this alone he is justified — put in the position of Christ. Now, God, "for Christ's sake," forgives and cleanses *the believer*. And that forgiveness and cleansing is an arrangement which is set up for a perpetual walk between God and His child.

And what is the purpose of this arrangement? To save? No! Jesus alone saves, and for His sake alone the Father forgives the child who has trusted Jesus. Forgiveness and cleansing are to bring about and promote *fellowship* between God and His child.

It is this fellowship about which John is writing. And fellowship is dependent on confession, forgiveness, and cleansing. And fellowship has mainly two great objectives: (1) joy, and (2) fruitfulness.

In the parable of the vine and the branches John talks about abiding in Christ as the means of fruitfulness. This abiding is fellowship. "If ye abide in me, and my words abide in you, ye shall ask what ye will, and it shall be done unto you" (John 15:7). And through that whole discussion he bears upon fruitfulness. Now, here in this first letter he is saying, "That which we have seen and heard declare we unto you, that ye also may have fellowship with us: and truly our fellowship is with the Father, and with his Son Jesus Christ. And these things write we unto you, that your joy may be full" (I John 1:3-4).

So, fellowship produces joy and fruitfulness in the believer. Fellowship is dependent on forgiveness and cleansing of the believer, and these in turn are dependent on the believer's confession of sins. Thus, it is an arrangement of a walk between the Father and His child.

It would be well to pause here and ask what is the difference between forgiveness and cleansing. Let us give an illustration. My little boy is mine by birth. Nothing else made him mine except birth. That is once for all established, and cannot be altered by anything I do or anything he does or anything anybody else does. So that settles that. I do not have to do anything to keep him being my child, nor does he. He is, and stays, my child, because he was born my child.

But, I want fellowship with him. I like to take him in my lap and fondle him, and make us both happy. This fellowship is necessary both for him and for me, if we are to be happy together.

Now, sometimes he likes to play in the mud. Even if he does, he still is my child. But I tell him to keep out of the mud, because when he is muddy I can't take him in my lap and love him as I want to. He knows I don't want him to play in the mud, but still, occasionally, he likes to. So, his mother and I are getting ready for a little trip. We have dressed him up, and he is clean and smells good. Now, while we are dressing in our best, he goes off and gets in the mud. When I call, "Son, where art thou?" as God called for Adam, he comes to me with mud all over him. I remind him of my will about this and ask him why he did it. His eyes gather tears, and he sobs out that he is sorry.

Immediately that does something to my heart. He is helpless. Nothing he can do can change things now. He stands before me in confession of his "sin," and wishes he could keep out of the mud as I want him to do. Now watch. His attitude takes away the offence. That is forgiveness. I had to assume, when he was born, responsibility for all his sins and failures. I alone am responsible. He is helpless. But his attitude clears up the whole offence so that fellowship is restored between us. My heart goes out to him in love, for I can bear it and he can not. I am, therefore, his sin-bearer, and I say to that penitent, confessing little boy, "It's all right, Son. You'll do better as long as you feel that way."

He has confessed, the offence is gone, and he is forgiven, but, he is still dirty. I have on my "holy" clothes; I cannot take him in my arms. What shall I do? He cannot cleanse himself, and I cannot take him up as he is. Then I must cleanse him from the defilement of mud. When he is cleansed he is ready for full fellowship with his father. No offence, no defilement.

The Greek words bring this out. The word for "forgiveness" means to send away, like when the offerer of the Old Testament put his hands on the offering and drove it away into the wilderness. "Remission" is another word for it. But the word for "cleansing" has to do with washing away defilement. Thus, "If we confess our sins, he is faithful and just to forgive us our sins, and to cleanse us from all unrighteousness."

Now, something else comes out in this passage. The mud on that little boy is not a part of him, nor of him. It is the defilement of the world. God's concern with a believer's sins is not judicial; it is remedial. The offence caused by my boy's disobedience and playing in mud is not an offence that might be committed against me by the boy of someone else. If my neighbor's boy threw a rock through my window, that offence would have to be dealt with by law, as far as I am concerned. Thus, he would have no recognition in my favor, but the act would have to stand in judgment under law. Whatever remedy should be applied to his sins must be applied by his father, not me. But in the case of my own boy, I have already assumed complete responsibility for all he does. Thus, when he damages his clothes or does anything else that causes expense to me, the bill is already paid. My whole concern about his sin now is remedial. The judicial part of it was settled when he was born my child.

So it is that when I was born God's child, the whole judicial aspect of my sins was settled, and I was pronounced by the law holy. Nothing I ever do can affect my relationship to God as His child. God is responsible for what I do and the debt of all my sins has been paid already. God's interest in my sins now is wholly remedial. What He wants is to keep me cleansed from the defilement of the old life, now dead but hanging on until the death of the body. This is where I touch the world, through the fleshly life, and this is where I become defiled. If I hate this defilement, and confess it before God, my attitude takes away the offence, and he forgives me. Then, through the blood of Christ, He lovingly washes away the defilement. Then I can have fellowship with Him. That will make me happy and help me bear fruit of the Spirit.

Notice again, the offence of sin in the life of God's child is not a breach of relationship. Relationship — father and child — depends on birth, and is forever settled on that ground. Fellowship — the *walk* of the father and child — depends on conduct. Relationship can never be broken; fellowship can. Our birth of the Spirit is brought about through repentance and faith in Christ as our complete and only Saviour. Once for all this is settled there. Our fellowship in the Spirit is brought about and kept by confession of sin on our part and forgiveness and cleansing on God's part. This is promoted throughout our walk with the Lord.

Furthermore, because we are God's children, we have the right, on confession of our sins, to forgiveness and cleansing. This is very important. Forgiveness and cleansing are not acts of God's mercy. The only mercy God has for any of us is in Jesus Christ. His act of mercy is giving Jesus to be our Sacrifice for all sin. Forgiveness and cleansing are acts of justice, based on the finished work of Christ for us. God has an agreement with our Advocate, that, if we will confess our sins, He will forgive. And this act of forgiveness and cleansing (for it is all one act) comes out of God's faithfulness and justice. He is faithful to His Son, according to agreement, and just in forgiving and cleansing us because of the blood. Therefore, "He is faithful and just to forgive us, and to cleanse us from all unrighteousness." All this wonderful life is brought to us through Jesus. Our Advocate works it all up there at the throne, and the Spirit works it all down here in our hearts. Praise His Holy Name!

CHAPTER VI

Walled Cities: The Sin Question (Continued)
Dealing With Sons

NOW THERE are several matters still dangling, and I hope I will not weary my reader if we pause here long enough to pick them up.

First, why is it God will not forgive His child until that child confesses his sins? If God has assumed all responsibility and has paid for all our sins, does He get offended when we sin against Him? No, God loves to the end. He is the ideal Father. He has been satisfied by the blood about our sins and cannot longer take offence at them. What, then, is the necessity for our confessing them before He forgives? Partly, it is for our benefit.

When I was a little boy we played near some thorn trees at the old school house. When we would stick a thorn in our bare feet, our teacher would insist on picking it out, often much to our displeasure. Why? Because if we left it, it would fester and might poison the whole system. So, if God lets us linger with an offence in our heart, if He fails to break that sin in us and bring us to penitence and humble confession, that sin will poison our whole system and break the fellowship that is so necessary for our growth. God is perfect; the offence will not hurt His character, but it will hurt ours. He loves us so much that He wants us to yield up anything that would mar our fellowship with Him.

Then, too, we must always keep in mind that God cannot tolerate sin. Either He must put sin out of the sinner, or put the sinner out of His fellowship; for He cannot run around with sin.

Another matter here is important. There is such a thing as a possibility of perpetual fellowship with God. Even though we sin, this fellowship can remain unbroken. The idea is expressed in John 1:7: "But if we walk in the light as he is in the light, we have fellowship one with another, and the blood of Jesus Christ his Son cleanseth us from all sin."

Now, what is it to walk in the light as He is in the light? Well, that means to have the same viewpoint that He has, the same attitude He has, and the same objective He has. We are to see ourselves as utter sinners, just as He does, and accept that as the final judgment of ourselves. When we do that, we eliminate all class distinctions, and all of us come down to one common base — sinners saved by Grace. Never can we rise from this basis, one above the other. Always it is and ever will be the same. Here is where we find our common fellowship. Anytime anybody looks upon another and thinks himself better than that one, he has broken the fellowship among believers. But if we see it this way, as God sees it, then we have fellowship one with another. This is seeing ourselves as we appear in the light of God, and just as He sees us.

Not only are we to have the same viewpoint that God has, but we are to have the same attitude. We must hate our sin. That is what the Spirit does, and if He be in us we will feel that hatred of our sins, unless we quench Him.

Then, our objective is the same as God's, to rid ourselves of sin and fleshly defilement, and to practice holiness. The old fleshly life, dead and decaying, is ever tied to us and will be so until we die. Its mind is always thinking unholy things, and its lust is ever desiring unholy things, and it produces nothing but defilement. While we tolerate its presence, we must ever be cleansed from it.

So, with God's viewpoint, and God's attitude, and God's objective, we can maintain a constant state of fellowship with Him. For, while we are in this kind of walk with God, "the blood of His Son, Jesus Christ, keeps on cleansing us (the verb is present action) from all sin." That is, though there be sin and imperfection and failure, sins of commission and of omission, or whatever of fleshly thoughts or even deeds transpire in our lives, if we have an open-hearted attitude about ourselves and our sins, we can know that the blood is cleansing. It is only when we have the channel blocked with a disposition of unwillingness to judge ourselves with God's judgment that we stop the flow of His cleansing blood.

Self-judgment is that which keeps us in fellowship. For, if we are willing to judge ourselves, we are not judged of God. If we come before the court and plead guilty, our Advocate is constantly handling our case. For always there will be sins to cleanse away, whether we notice them or not. Walking in the light, as He is in the light, will make us more conscious of them, will increase our hatred for them, and unite us in God's objective to overcome them and grow in His grace. With this attitude God can produce the fruit of the Spirit in us.

The sum of what we have said here is that unbroken fellowship with God does not depend on unbroken sinlessness, but upon unbroken willingness to confess and judge our sins. This is walking in the light.

Of course, we must remember that sin, as we speak of it, does not consist only in rash outbreaks of temper, vile language, insult to another, or any other positive act of sin. Neither is it limited to just laziness or general sins of omission. It is a sin to form connections or alliances in this world with those who are unfriendly to God. It is sinful to be where God would not have you be; to have any life which would not be His life shared; to let anything linger in your heart without judgment against it, if it be sinful contemplation. We cannot keep from being defiled by the flesh, but we can keep the cleansing process going on. Sin comes in ten thousand varieties, and there is always some unholy demon knocking at our door. It is not enough to keep him outside, but we should not even stand and chat pleasantly with him. Thus, we see, sin is ever upon us, and walking in the light will so reveal it as to make us cry out with Jonah, "Salvation is of the Lord."

Again, does a believer ever get so he will not confess sin? Certainly. We may grow cold, and starved, and neglectful of our Christian lives. In that state we may fall into temptations which will bring us into heinous sin. It is not likely that one who has crossed Jordan in surrender, who lives in this mature understanding of faith, will refuse to confess sin. But the wilderness wanderers almost universally will do it. What then is the remedy God proposes for that attitude? Just exactly what He did for Israel and what He has done for all His sinning children! Just exactly what any good father would do for a stubborn child. Chastisement! The Lord loves His children so much that He will not let them go beyond the reach of His chastening rod. "Whom the Lord loveth he chasteneth, and scourgeth every son whom he receiveth."

For what does God chasten His child? Because He is offended and angry? No, because He loves His child. Once my son thought I was rather hard on him. He grew sullen because I would not let him have all the privileges he wanted. One morning as he left for school in a sullen mood, I called him to me and opened the Bible at Hebrews 12:6 and let him read it. He reflected a moment, smiled, and went away with a lighter heart.

Then, does God chasten to make us pay for sin? If my son burns the house down, do I beat him and refuse to forgive him until he has paid for the house? Certainly not! I assumed all such responsibility when he was born. As far as he is concerned the house is paid for. My only reason for chastising him is to improve his character and bring him into more obedient fellowship with me.

Now, all children properly cared for have to come, at some time and in some manner, under the chastening rod. For chastening is not only to take something out of us, but also to put holiness into us. (This we cannot discuss here. We have been dealing with the matter of offences and the failure to confess them). It is always "for our profit." I know of no child of God who can hold out against God's chastening. Thus, our loving Father breaks down the rebellion in us and brings us to penitence and confession. He has never yet lost a case.

Another question is, what if I die with a sin unconfessed? This is very important and terribly misunderstood. First, let us remember that forgiveness and cleansing are not necessary to save, but are for the saved, and for them only. Nobody can be forgiven a single sin until he has

a Saviour to take that sin. So, no lost man is ever forgiven. Only when He trusts the Saviour can God take
away a single sin. Hence, forgiveness and cleansing are
not for the lost, but for the saved. Second, let us remember
that forgiveness and cleansing are for the express purpose
of bringing about and promoting fellowship between God
and His child. Furthermore, fellowship does not save, but
is for the definite purpose of bringing joy and fruitfulness
to the believer. This is what we mean by growth in grace.

So, sin — unconfessed sin — is all that can break fellowship. This takes away the joy of salvation and mars its
fruitfulness. But this sin does not break our relationship to
God. So, a sinning believer is God's child but out of fellowship with Him. Suppose he dies in that state?

Suppose my boy rebels against my will and, for the time,
becomes stubborn and will not confess his sin? During
that time he starts across the street, and a car strikes him
and crushes his body there on the street. He is dead. I
look out there and see it all happen, but, because he is out
of fellowship with me, do you think I refuse to go out and
pick up his body and claim him as my child? Of course
not! With a heart that loved him in his sin just as in his
fellowship, I pick his broken body up and tenderly bring it
into the house. Dead though he be in body, we are in
fellowship now. Nothing is between us.

And so, if a believer, in a stubborn and rebellious moment, should die, death puts away all the offence — the
flesh — and God's child is at once home with his Father,
and in eternal fellowship. This is what we are all coming
to one day if we belong to Him.

Death brings complete fellowship. Actually, that is what *confession* is. It is pleading guilty before the court and taking a death sentence on our sin before our Father. We thus submit to death. In Christ our sin is put away, and we are "made nigh by the blood of the cross." So, if I die in a sinful moment, God has me, and that old, troublesome sin question is over forever. What wonders our God has performed for us in Jesus Christ our Saviour!

There is but one more question to which we give attention here. That is the age-old question, "If there is no danger of my ever being lost after I am saved, why can't I just 'turn loose' and sin all I want to?"

The answer is easy. When God saves a man he tears down all the fences around him, removes him from under the law, and controls him wholly by the Spirit. He puts His Holy Spirit in the believer's heart, and that Spirit hates sin. He is there to make the believer conscious of sin and to hate sin. When you find a professing Christian who loves sin, put a question mark there.

I have heard a number of times this old story. A colored preacher had been preaching that when we are once saved we are always saved. One of his hearers said to him: "If I believed like you preaches, I'd jes' go out an' sin all I pleases." The preacher replied, "Brother Jones, don't you sin all you wants to?" After a moment of reflection, the brother replied, "Yassuh, mo' dan I wants to."

This is the answer. If you are a child of God, no matter what progress you have made in holiness, you sin more than you want to. And that is true of all children of God. The difference between a lost man and a saved man is, the lost man sins and loves it, but the saved man sins and hates it.

The hog loves mud, and will wallow in it every time it can. The sheep hates mud, and even though it may fall into it, it will get out at once and seek to get the mud off. This is the difference between a lost man and a saved man. Saved men are more conscious of sin than are lost men, because the Spirit is in the saved man making him conscious of sin. But the saved man hates his sin and judges it with his Father, while the lost man loves his sin and hates the Father. Thus the saved man walks in fellowship and receives cleansing, while the lost man piles up offences against himself to await judgment at the last great day.

Yes, most believers sin all they want to, and more. They wish they could sin less. John teaches that in his first letter all along. It is in the tense of his verbs. Translating I John 3:9 literally, we have, "Whosoever is born of God does not continue in the practice of sin; for his seed remaineth in him, and he cannot continue in the practice of sin, because he is born of God." Falling into sin and getting out and confessing it is a far different thing from continuing in the practice of sin. When you see a professor continuing in sin you may safely say that he is not a possessor. God's children tend toward godliness. If they do not, God's chastening hand may help out. If these be not evident it is likely that God has nothing to do with the case.

This has been a long discussion. I hope my reader is not too weary to go on to the two other realms of strongholds which we must attack. In this discussion we have shown that *God does everything for the believer;* that the believer can no more handle the sin question after being saved than he could before. So, God has considered every need, and has met them all in Christ Jesus, the Saviour and Deliverer.

What then is the believer to do? A sentence or two will answer that. The key word is "YIELD" (Rom. 6:12,13). "Do not let sin reign in your mortal body, that ye should obey it in the lusts thereof." Meaning this, "Do not let yourself be ruled by sin, for you have died as a sinner. There is now a new way of life. You will always have sin, but it need not rule over you. God has provided a way of escape from its rule. Find out the truth about His great provision and step out into the freedom of the Spirit. You will find that you are no longer in bondage to sin, for the sin question has been settled, and there is an answer for every need in Jesus Christ. Therefore, do not yield yourself to sin. Yield yourself to God, and tell the devil that Christ has broken the chain that bound you. You have found freedom in Christ, and you are going to live now like a man who is alive from the dead."

Thus, in utter faith that this is true, trust in God and go on unto maturity. This long explanation is to help you to see the truth just declared — that there is a complete answer to sin. The truth shall make you free.

CHAPTER VII

Walled Cities: Life's Sorrows and Trials

BEFORE we take up the next stronghold to be attacked, let us review our principle. We have dealt with the sin question and found that sin could not be eradicated. We found also that we could not restrain it by sheer will power. We found that victory over sin did not consist in getting rid of sin, but in coming to understand that it had been dealt with completely in the blood of Christ. Thus we accepted, on pure faith, that "sin shall not have dominion over" us, for "we are not under law, but under grace." Sin will not be our judge or exercise rule over us, for we are dead to sin, and "he that is dead is freed from sin." No more, therefore, shall it ever bring its judgment upon us, and we take that on pure faith in God's Word.

We found that God's concern about our sins now, under grace, is not a matter of paying for sin, for that was done by our Saviour. His purpose now is to keep the man who is alive unto God through Christ washed and free from defilement from the old dead sinner, and thus make him fit for fellowship with God. Hence, God's dealing with our sins now is purely remedial, and has as its purpose purifying and maturing us into godliness in experience. This, like the matter of dealing with the penalty of sin, has already been taken care of in the Cross, and is to be applied to our lives by the Spirit here and the Advocate there, the Spirit making us hate and confess sins here, and Jesus putting away our sins there. Hence, we must trust the whole problem to Him and not struggle in the energy of the flesh to overcome. It is a fight of faith to the finish. "The just shall live by faith." So, as we trust and confess our sins, God works His cleansing and holiness in us day by day. If we become rebellious and do not confess our sins, He chastens us into obedience, so that He can perform His godliness in us. Thus, under grace, "He dealeth with us as with sons."

We have shown that God has a complete remedy for all phases of sin, and that we can trust Him completely to do what He purposes in us. Only, we must be yielded to Him and, at all costs, permit His work to go on in us. The believer must take this all on absolute faith before he will see any results. That is what we tell the lost sinner he must do before he can feel that he is saved; that is what the believer must do before he can enter this Promised Land.

One important thing: If you yield the matter to God in faith, don't take it back just because you don't see any great results. God may test your faith by waiting. Keep on saying: "Lord, the best I can I have yielded this whole problem to you, and I am counting on you to be doing now what I have trusted you to do for me. I am helpless; you are mighty. You are the Great Physician; I am the patient. I am leaving my case in your hands. Whatever happens now will be your responsibility." If you trust this way, in His own time and way God will work His purposes in your life. Believe it, and go on.

Now, let us come to the next great stronghold which we must attack by faith, namely, our trials and burdens.

How can we overcome life's trials, heartaches, sorrows, doubts, and fears, with all their human complications?

Let us say, first of all, that our burdens and trials are not crosses. I used to hear good brethren, in their testimony meetings, recite their trials and hardships. Often they would conclude humbly, "But I suppose that these are my crosses, and I must bear them." That is wrong. Crosses are not burdens, they are the only God-given means to put an end to burden.

I have studied the cross from its earliest history. So far as I can find, a cross was never used for any purpose other than to die on. It was never a burden to be laid upon the back of any man for punishment or discipline. It has only one idea in view, and that is the death of its victim. And the one use, as far as the believer is concerned, for the Cross of Christ, is the death of self. "If any man will come after me, let him deny himself, and take up his cross daily, and follow me" (Luke 9:23).

Here lies an important truth. Death is God's way out of sin. That is the only way we can ever settle the sin question, that is, to die out of it. That is what we have meant in our treatment of sin: the sinner must repent, consent to death, plead guilty and take the judgment of the court; for that is what repentance is. And John's baptism of repentance — going down into the water — was the symbol of death. It signified both a consent of death to the unregenerate man inside and to the final death of the body. That is why a believer has to die in the body, to get rid of sin. Otherwise, when one is saved, God could take him home that way. So, the Cross is the instrument of death, both of the sinful nature in us, and of the body. Thus, death is our only way out of sin, and the Cross is that instrument of death. So, we must take our cross daily in experience and die daily, just as we died in faith under the law when we first trust Jesus the Saviour. So we must come at last to the grave where sin in the body is left forever.

Now, if we are to realize this death in our experience here as believers, we must be continually nailing self to the Cross. Only, we ourselves cannot do it, but we can submit ourselves to the Cross and let God do it, as we have been teaching.

The whole problem in bearing our burdens is putting self on the Cross. We must know the truth, and the truth shall make us free. How shall we bring the Cross into our experiences on this point? I shall try to answer fully.

There is no doubt that the world is full of burdens and heartache. We struggle with hunger, with thirst, with all the passions and desires of the flesh. In our weakness we sin and find ourselves the victims of our sins. The world is greedy and selfish, and it is difficult for us to live honestly. Then there is sickness and death and war and strife and lack and need and every conceivable condition to make life unhappy. Then there are personal problems, like family complications, disobedience of children, and, as we facetiously say sometimes, trouble with both out-laws and in-laws. This is not a good world. Paul called it "this present evil world." And he indicated that God had no purpose of fixing it up and reforming it, but that He sent Jesus Christ to "save us out of" this present evil world. So, there isn't much hope that it will be any better.

The reason is obvious: The same people who produced it are now its doctors. The same distorted order of life which man, out of self, has brought about characterizes his remedy for our ills. How can man who, in selfishness and greed, has set up an intolerably sinful world bring, out of the same heart, a remedy for its ills? It has been judged by Jesus Christ, the only good Man who ever walked in its midst, and the disposition of that world toward goodness was expressed in His crucifixion. Thus, the believer will find that this world has no place for him, and he might as well prepare to get out of it.

Now, if any civic club optimist doubts that this is a bad world, let him make a list of the governments that have absolutely refused Christ — and that is all of them; of the wars that have been fought, and the millions of people who are still sharing their tragedy; of the business in which intelligent men are engaged making war munitions, trying to invent a better killer, and on and on with the endless efforts to bring greater destruction; of the doctors and nurses and hospitals of innumerable types and specialties that are necessary to treat human ills; of the religions that offer a "way of life," among which are so many false remedies; of the penitentiaries and jails, the various asylums and institutes for the handicapped, both mental and physical; of the orphanages, courts of law, law-making bodies, police, patrols, and the corrupt uses of all these institutions of law and order; of the array of drives and campaigns to soothe and heal human ills; and, skipping over a thousand other things, take a look at the graveyards, with their scenes of crying and sorrow and parting and death. Then ask who did all this to our world. The answer is, man! How could such a man build a good world?

Well, the conclusion is that if anybody tries to live a life different from what this world offers, he will have a hard time. So said Jesus, and so said the inspired Apostles.

"They have hated me, they will hate you." "They that would live godly in Christ Jesus must suffer persecution." Not only, then, shall we fall a victim to the common sorrows of this world, in which all have a part, but we shall be persecuted by this world if we try to follow Christ. How shall we find the answer to all this? How can the Cross help us here?

In the first place, self will have to face a matter of justice and say, "After all, it is no more than I deserve." If it were not for the grace and mercy of a loving God, we would all not only suffer the common ills of this world but would spend eternity in an endless hell of torment. That is the just deserts of self. That is what is coming to us, if God does not intervene. So, if we suffered all these things, it would be no more than we deserve, and God would be entirely just in leaving us to our own chosen way of life with its sorrow.

With this conclusion we start even and without any complaints against God. We cannot blame anybody but ourselves for the world we have built. God did not do it. We cannot blame our choice of life on anyone but ourselves. God admonished man to choose to obey Him, and man himself chose otherwise. All that we suffer in this life is simply the natural result of our choice. Strange to say, men of all generations, though aware of this world's sorrows and their own contribution to it, will still choose against God. We can blame nobody but ourselves for our world and its sorrows and heartaches. That is sad, but it is true. So, here we stand, with our own hearts laden with our own self-produced burdens, and must accept them as a matter of sheer justice, and nothing more.

This is our first truth which we seek to bring to the believer's mind. It ought to end all complaining, even there, when we see it. And if we accept that as true, without complaint, that is putting self on the the Cross. Self is that one which whimpers and complains at its hard lot in this world. But when we see that self brought it upon us, there is nothing to do except to put self on the Cross and say, "Stop your complaining; you are the one who made this world! You must submit to what you have done and blame no one but yourself." This is dying in self to start with, and using the Cross for its intended purpose in our lives. Consent to the death and find relief.

By way of illustration, let us say someone has hurt your feelings, and because of this you have a burden. It may be that they have imposed and have been very unjust. It may be that they have done you great injury, and, by human standards, ought to make amends. But suppose they do not. How can you ease your burden about this? First, looking at it from God's viewpoint, it is nothing more than you deserve anyway. You helped build this world; it is now merely back-firing on you. That in itself is enough to settle the matter. But, if you are a believer in Christ, the debt has been paid by His blood. He suffered your reproach, so your bill is paid. So, if you send up a bill for hurt pride, it is paid already.

All that can get hurt in anybody is pride. There is nothing else to hurt. It is that little deity — self — which we have put up on a throne, but who, because of its sinfulness, has no right to reign anywhere. When somebody else has a little god competing with yours, and theirs gets the best of the battle, that does not matter, for both of them combine to be that which crucified the Lord of glory.

And since Jesus has paid that bill on the cross, the Lord will not now pay any attention to the complaints of a dead man. Once for all every injustice that will ever be done to us in this world has been paid for in the cross. "Jesus paid it all; all to Him we owe." *There is no ground, absolutely none, on which a believer has any right to take offence.* We must simply call every reproach square under the blood, and thank God that that is true. This truth will make you free insofar as you will accept it.

Now, granting that this is a bit stoical, it is also quite spiritual. It may require faith and prayer and the Holy Spirit to practice this truth, but this is what we need. However, we come now to a little more hopeful look at our trials. And that is the great prospect of becoming stewards of them.

Whereas, "the way of the transgressor" is justly hard, and we have suffered merely the just recompense for our misdeeds and have nothing to complain of, we find God has provided for us to make a blessing out of our trials. Instead of merely reaping what we sow, we find our Father saying, through the Apostle Paul, "All things work together for our good." Thus God reveals to us a way to make judgment become chastening for our good, stumbling stones to become stepping stones, and one who "labors and is heavy laden" to find "glory in tribulations."

This is wonderful! To be forced merely to admit that we get what is coming to us, when we reap the tragedy and sorrow of the world we have built, is like telling a child who is already made sad by his misdeeds and their sad results, "I told you so!" It is true, but it doesn't help much. But here is the Lord of all trial, "who endured the cross, despised the shame, and is set down at the right hand of God," telling us that the whole picture of our lives is changed. That which was once our curse now becomes our blessing. "All things" which once were merely the sad results of our sin now become that which "works together for our good." With the Cross He turned His trial into glory; now He tells us we can do the same.

So, here comes the Deliverer to walk with us every day, to see that we turn defeat into victory, and we find Him to be the same great Saviour who put us to death as sinners under the law and raised us up as children of God under grace. Blessed be His Name!

In dealing with the sin question we were told not to strive in the energy of the flesh against our sins but to submit them in sorrow and confession as our sinful plight before the Lord, and, not only to ask Him to do something about the malignancy but also to believe that He does exactly what we trust Him to do. We were to yield to Him the whole matter and believe that He would take care of it. Now, here are our burdens and trials, and the Deliverer is here to help us. What shall we do with them?

Shall we try to get rid of our burdens and trials? That is the first thing the flesh suggests. It recommends that we begin immediately to solve the problem by getting free from it. If it be, for instance, a problem of home life, the flesh suggests remedies to be obtained in the best world sources—maybe the help of a psychologist, a psychiatrist, or a welfare worker or lawyer. It may be that all of these can be used to advantage at one time or another, but this is not the place to start. Above all things, consult God first. Pray over it and ask Him to show you His will.

Every situation is its own problem, and there can be no way of stating rules about one that will apply to another.

Remember, you are God's child, in a world of sin, and you do not know the way. Jesus is the way, the truth, and the life, and you will need Him in all three entities.

So, the first conclusion about your problem is, *don't try to get rid of it* until you have looked into it thoroughly. If, after you have submitted it to God, He takes it away, all right. But it may be something He has permitted to come into your life to bless you. Don't handle it rashly. Remember, you have trusted all to Him; now try to practice it. It is His business, and His alone, now, what happens to you. You may be contradicting His plans and thus robbing yourself of the great blessing He has for you.

We cannot over-emphasize this principle. When you cross Jordan you have surrendered all to Him. Now keep dependent on Him, and move only at His direction. When you don't know what to do, wait until the pillar of cloud and fire moves on.

If God is going to work His character in us, He must begin with tribulation. Trials are the common lot of His children, for in them is our spiritual education wrought. The children of Israel had not been long across the Red Sea until they came into a desert place where they were seized with a thirst for water. God permitted this so that they might learn that He could turn their trial into something good. It is easy for us to see how something we call good can be good for us; but how can the adverse things work together for our good? The secret is that that which pleases us merely keeps us like we are; that which is unpleasant to us may serve to change us.

And here comes a great lesson. God is not trying to change His ways to suit us; He is trying to change us to suit His ways. Since we are wrong, and He is right, anything that simply satisfies our fleshly tastes and desires will not help us because it brings no change in us. The flesh will never love Jesus. Nobody likes to walk the way of Christ while the flesh dictates his likes and dislikes.

When the children of Israel hit this desert place they cried for water. And when they found water they found that water to be bitter. God told Moses to cut a certain tree and cast it in the water. When he did this, the water became sweet. This tree is Christ's Cross symbolized. Its lesson here is the difference between suffering for a purpose and just suffering. The Cross puts meaning into suffering and helps the believer to endure that which is unpleasant to the flesh and makes it become a joy in the Spirit.

Let me illustrate: I step into a hospital ward, and there I see two women, one lying in each bed, both in great suffering. To one I say, "Tell me, what is your trouble?" She replies that she has been burned. I ask her how it happened. She tells me that she was lying in bed, drunk, and smoking a cigarette. The bed caught on fire and before she was rescued she was nearly burned to death. She confesses she was to blame, and for her own sin and carelessness she suffers.

I turn to the other woman, who suffers likewise, and ask her how she was burned. Under great stress of pain she tells me that while she was outside her house it caught on fire. She rushed upstairs to rescue her little daughter, and though she was able to wrap the little girl in blankets and get her safely out, she herself was badly burned. But, instead of the sad conclusion that it was her sin and carelessness that brought her calamity upon her, she looks across the room and beckons a sweet little girl to her bedside.

"But," she says, "I would endure it all again to save my baby." And as the little girl nestles close to her mother, trying to understand, there is a deep satisfaction in that mother's soul which makes pain worth while.

So, there is a difference between just suffering, and suffering for a purpose. One woman had just suffered; the other had put a cross into her suffering. Now, if we can see that our pains are for a purpose, and, furthermore, if we can find that all we endure in this life is for our spiritual good rather than a misfortune to us, we can, like Paul, arrive at that place where we "take pleasure in tribulations," knowing that God has in them a purpose for our good and His glory. That understanding will shut out the cry of the flesh, and give meaning to our trials.

And so this brings us to an important principle: faith is not to get rid of our trials; it is to help us use them for *our good* and *God's glory*.

Why does God leave a believer in this world? If we are eternally saved, why does not God take us home and save us from the struggle in this world of sin? The answer is twofold: (1) This is God's proving ground, where He works His character in us. The self life must be dealt with, and here amidst the trials of life He perfects us through His sanctifying grace. (2) He wants us to be His witnesses so that others may be turned to Him.

Strangely enough, it is through the same trials that He does both. However, in this chapter we are concerned primarily with the former reason.

It is certain that God must do somehing in us before He can do anything through us. That work which He does in us we call sanctification. It is a process which continues all through our journey here on earth, and it consists in putting off the old man and putting on the new. In the matter of outward conduct, it tends to reduce sinful habits and sinful acts and produces a conduct of godliness. However, this is the result, and not the cause, of something that has gone on inside, namely, the realization that we have turned from dependence upon the flesh to the help of the Spirit and have thus been enabled to produce a better outward conduct. Desires within have changed, which show outwardly. Association with sin, which once was our pleasure, now becomes a problem which we despise, while association with God, which once seemed dull and dreary to us, now has become our chief joy. The crossing of Jordan is that place in the believer's life where he ceases to yearn for the flesh pots of Egypt and begins to desire the old corn of the land.

How does God produce this character within us? First, by giving us an enlarged concept of the life which is ours, and second, by giving us an enlarged concept of the God which is ours.

We have been born of God for eternal living. But the carnal believer lives still as though he had been born for this life only. His estimate of property value, social standing, earthly ambitions, and all that concerns this life marks him as one who is worldly in his understanding of life. The new life — eternal life — must now be worked into his experience. So God suits the experiences of his life so as to wean him from earth and promote heavenly mindedness.

In order to do this He lets the believer come into numerous and varied problems and trials to teach him that nothing in this world endures, and that he cannot pin his hopes upon anything in this world.

Andrew Fuller in one of his great classic sermons tells a story which has often been used as an illustration of this truth. The great eagle of the western mountains, he says, builds her nest high in the crags of the Rockies. When the young eaglets are large enough to fly, they are very lazy and will not try their wings. The wise old mother eagle fills the nest with rocks and sticks to make it uncomfortable for her young, so they will want to exercise their wings in flight, and thus get ready for their natural altitude in the sky. It was thus, he says, that God filled Israel's nest in Egypt with trials, that His people might want to leave the accursed place and start for home. So were all the trials along the way designed to produce a continual dissatisfaction in them, to urge them on and on to the land of promise. God wants His children to get a larger concept of life; so He takes away our earthly supports, and shows us that nothing here endures. Thus He turns our eyes to a longer view of things and makes us dissatisfied with this present existence. When we find nothing here to satisfy our longing for permanence, He calls upon us to look heavenward and see the things which He has prepared for them that love Him.

When we see that God has planned a longer life for us than just this earthly existence, things that seemed large to us, because they were set in this short span, now become little when set in the eternal span. A mountain may loom large before us when we are standing at its foot. But when we stand on a higher peak and fit that mountain into the chain that fades away into the blue, it will look small and of little importance. Thus it is that God, through trial, gives us the longer view of life. And when we see that we are going to live forever, that trial which seemed so difficult and complex at the moment becomes, from a higher view, a mere insignificant step on the way to eternity. Other events of far greater importance submerge it in the long chain of experiences by which God leads us on to the things eternal.

Another thing trial does for us: it gives us patience to wait on God. "Tribulation worketh patience." But why do we need patience? Because we are not going to arrive at life's great goal as soon as we first expected. Youth is very eager to get there, and takes all the short cuts possible. But age and experience bring a maturity which lengthens our view of life, and we see that God has more in prospect for us than this short life here. So we are taught by trial to have patience and wait on the Lord. If this life is all God had to offer us, we would be justified in being a bit impatient and setting great store by securing all the favors it has to offer. But God has something beyond all compare with this earth to offer us, so He tempers us with things that bring us low and hold us back so that we can with patience wait for the glories He has prepared for us.

There is much more struggling for expression here, but let us sum it up by saying that God uses all of life's trials to mature us into His view of things, so that we can put away our childish ambitions and look at life through eternal eyes. This lengthens our view of life, enlarges the prospects of its ends, and teaches us the necessary patience to wait until God is ready to reveal its glory.

Well, if we are to live such a long life, and find it to have such glorious prospects, we need a *closer view of the God of eternal life*. So, the second thing God does in sanctifying us is to give us a greater concept of our God.

Jesus was out on the little sea with His disciples when a great storm suddenly whipped down the valley and across the waters. Jesus was asleep in the stern of the ship. They hastily aroused Him, complaining, "Master, carest thou not that we perish?"

Here is the flesh with its first concern — self. What if we do perish? It is no more than we deserve. It is the wilderness wanderer that is always crying out for self-comfort and self-satisfaction. When a soldier is sent on a dangerous mission, does he say to his commanding officer, "Carest thou not that I perish?" Who are we to tell Jesus that He must see that we do not perish? That is His business. You hear people excusing themselves from dereliction of duty. They haven't time, they claim; after all, one has to live. Well, who said so? We have to die; that is certain. But who said we had to live? In fact, if we are not living in the purposes of God, and are rebellious toward Him, the world would be better off if we were not living at all. No, to live is not the prime consideration. To do God's will is all that matters.

Despite the fact that these disciples had left all and followed Him, they were concerned with the preservation of self, and complained that the Master was careless. They did not understand that this storm might be the very thing that would introduce them to a deeper understanding of their Master.

He calmed the waves. We might have expected Him to say, "Boys, I am glad you aroused me. That was a terrible storm and might have drowned us all." But His only comment was upon their faith. It was as if He were saying, "Boys, I was going to show you something here, but, in your desire for the preservation of self, you missed the big show. Yes, I can command the waves, and that astounds you. I have all power. But if you had trusted me, you would have been able to see me sleep through a storm and ride the waves in all serenity; for no storm ever overturns the boat in which the Son of Man rides."

Which brings us to see: It is a great thing to see Jesus calm our storms; but it is a far greater blessing to us to see Him ride them. And, when our problems and trials fall upon us and we go asking God to get rid of them, we may be asking Him to take away that which He has permitted in order to reveal His glory to us. *Faith is not to calm the storm; faith is to calm us in the storm.* Faith is not the solution to our problems in that it takes them away; faith is the solution *to us,* in that it enlarges our vision of our Lord and helps us to enter into His purposes. If we find out that nothing can harm us as long as we are in the boat with Jesus; that He has ridden all the storms that ever beset us and is seated the Victor over them all at the Father's right hand; we must surely believe that whatever He permits to come upon us is best, and we are to let it remain until He takes it out of the way at His own good will and pleasure.

So, one reason why we must be good stewards of our trials is that they may be the very door *through which we are introduced to a greater God*. The disciples had seen Jesus cure diseases, cast out demons, and do many other remedial miracles. They thought of Him as somebody who could take all the unpleasant things out of the way. But had they trusted Him here they would have been introduced to a God who not only could remove problems and trials, but *could endure* them. It is a much greater Christian who can endure trials than is he who can get rid of them. Jesus could have escaped the Cross if He had wanted to disobey His Father's will; but He could not have had the joy set before Him where He is now exalted at the right hand of God. You and I may be able to escape our burdens and trials to some extent, if we will shirk duty and stay out of God's will, but we will not get a vision of that greater God if we do. Who would not walk in the fiery furnace, if in so doing they can walk with a God who can nullify the power of fire to burn? Trial is the one great place to get acquainted with our Lord, for "he was a man of sorrows and acquainted with grief." It is there we find Him in His greatest power and glory.

Often in facing life's problems we are inclined to pit the wisdom of the flesh against the miracle of God. If we make God a competitor of the lights of this world, He will always shine more brightly than will they, but we shall never see Him in His full glory until all the lights of this world are shut out. It is only in our helplessness, when nothing else in this world will do, that we get our best vision of God, and see Him in His full glory. We must not, therefore, be afraid to enter into the shadows of this life, in trial or pain, for in there, somewhere, we will discover our Lord to be much more glorious than He would be in removing our trials.

We shall never become dissatisfied with our littleness until we see God in His greatness. We shall never want to throw away the works of the flesh until we have seen Him performing works of the Spirit.

If Martha had taken time to sit at the Master's feet long enough to discover the Christ in His heart, she would have been more concerned about setting before Him a feast of worship than a feast of victuals for His body. Her

offering would have been much more appropriate. As it
was, not having time to sit before Him, she reduced Him
to a household god and worked herself into a frenzy trying
to satisfy her own lowly concept of Him. She was alarmed
to learn that "but one thing was needful," and that it was
not that which had so consumed her in these precious
hours. But Mary took time to look into His face and
listen to His words, and she saw "Him that is invisible"
deep in his heart. Nothing but worship was appropriate
for this God. It takes yoke-walking to discover this.

If God is to work His character in us He must draw us
away from the ideal of the world and set our vision upon
the Ideal of Heaven. Like the boy in the "Great Stone
Face" story, we are put where we can look upon Him
until His character, revealed to us in our diverse trials, is
stamped indelibly upon our hearts, so that we can never
be satisfied to be anything short of what He is. This puts
to naught the lusts of the flesh and makes us scorn what
we are.

It is this concept of God which makes us tire so easily
of the handiwork of man in the modern church life. We
can understand how the worldling, who has never seen
the Lord through eyes that can see the "invisible," has
nothing to offer that will reach the heart, and thus, the
appeal of so much of our religion today is to the fancy of
the natural mind. Though we bring them to a profession
of faith in Christ, so often the vision quickly fades away,
for it had no depth.

You see, God wants to bind us to Him so that we will
never be attracted away by other gods. He wants us to live
as if we were citizens of eternity, not time, and to be
directed by the wisdom of Heaven, not of earth.

Religion is not a thing we can tack on to our lives as something to resort to in an emergency. Christ must be the God of the whole life, and nothing of either a temporal or eternal nature must be done without consulting His wisdom and being guided by His Spirit. For "Christ must be Lord of all or He is not Lord at all." Thus He must put us where we shall find the failure of the flesh in order to turn us to Him completely. For this reason He must let us down where nobody else but God can help us.

Peter walked upon the water as long as he depended on Christ. But when he looked at the waves and began to reason by the way things looked that there was danger, he began to sink. Was Jesus going to let him drown? Not at all. But He was going to teach Simon Peter that he was walking on Him, not on the water. When Peter got down to the neck and cried, "Lord, save, or I perish," then Christ raised him up. God often lets us sink in our trials up to the neck in order to kill in us any hope that the flesh can save. Thus we are turned to faith in Him alone.

Jonah cast his course in the wisdom of the flesh, but when he was thrown overboard he realized he had come to the end of his resources. He expected to drown, and, if nobody else had had an interest in the affair, his expectations would have been entirely correct. That is why we keep saying that the work of God is supernatural and has to do with the things which are impossible with men. Only in such cases can God demonstrate His great power, when the power of man has reached its extremity. So, when Jonah was thrown overboard, he had come to an end of the wisdom of the flesh. He might have thought now that it were better to go with God to Nineveh than to dive into the ocean by himself. And he would have been right. It is always better to go with God anywhere He leads than to go anywhere else alone. But God was not ready to destroy his servant; He just had to get Jonah where he could not resort to human wisdom so that He could show Jonah His almighty power.

Down in the big fish Jonah had time to think things over. First, why didn't he die down there? How could a man live without oxygen? Why didn't the big fish digest him? How long could he live down there? I imagine things got pretty literal down there. Three days and nights is a long time to sit there in a floundering fish, with gastric juices flowing all around him, still not dying. From the description of the record, water, seaweed, and all the things of the ocean came upon Jonah, and that fish took quite a trip down into the valleys of the sea. Yes, he was conscious and prayed unto God out of the "belly of hell." Jonah says, "I cried by reason of mine affliction unto the Lord." Sure, he got where only God could help him. Then when he cried, the Lord heard him. "When my soul fainted within me I remembered the Lord." That is just what it takes to get some of us to remember the Lord.

People get along fine until trouble comes. Many of our professing Christians, maybe they are real, go along and ignore the church. They fall into sin and compromise their stand, carrying a haughty head as if they had no further use for the Christ whom they professed. Pastors plead with them and try every way to induce them to a restoration of fellowship, but to no avail. Pastors are always waiting on some rebellious church members until trouble comes. As soon as it comes, they come for the preacher. The crowd they have been running with can't help them. It takes more solemn measures now. They don't go to the bridge club, the dance hall, the cocktail lounge, the clubs and societies of the world. They want somebody who more nearly represents the presence of God. The vilest sinners will do this. Only when we get where we have to have God will we turn and call for Him. This is too often true in the lives of the best of us.

God has a bad city over there, Nineveh, which needs preaching to bring them to repentance. So He must bring Jonah into an acquaintance with Him that leaves no doubt in the prophet's mind that "salvation is of the Lord" — of Him alone and of nobody else. Thus Jonah comes up with the knowledge of a God who can go down into the grave and come up from the dead, and he is sure that kind of a God can handle the wicked city of Nineveh.

Now, I don't believe that journey through the mountains and valleys of the sea proved to be any south sea island vacation trip for Jonah. It was a trial of death and resurrection. But it transformed the prophet's life by giving him a first hand acquaintance with a God he could never have found sailing around in boats on top of the water.

God wants us to know Him. And the greater are His purposes in us the deeper into the oceans of trouble and despair He will lead us, until we have been assured that God is far greater than we ever dreamed He was. We have to see God in sorrow and trial, in storm and strife, in adverse winds and turbulent seas, in the underground pathways where the lights of the world go out, to see Him in His majesty and glory. This brings sanctifying effects in us.

And what are these sanctifying effects? They are summed up in this: The gods of self perish and we are made to cry,

"The Lord our God is one God." When we see God in trial, we see Him in a glory that blinds us forever to the gods of pleasure. Thus the flesh and its lusts are defeated. They are blacked out by His blinding glory, like the mid-day sun was eclipsed by the light that shone from Heaven on Saul of Tarsus as he traveled to Damascus. We can't be satisfied to go back to a little god when our eyes "have beheld the King." This brings real progress in the believer's life. God puts us in the dark places so He can stamp His image so indelibly upon our hearts that we cannot turn again to the dim negatives of the sun-streaked gods of this world. This is working His character in us.

That is why we should be good stewards of our trials, and, by yielding to God's way, make them count for all God has intended in them. In my young life I was greatly impressed by one of God's servants to whom came a sudden trial of great bereavement. He prayed a simple prayer in three parts: (1) He said, in substance, "Lord, I do not question your providence. Just give me the grace to bear whatever you permit." (2) He said, "Lord, Help me to understand what you are trying to say to me in this trial." (3) He said, "Lord, help me to be a good witness in this trial, and let the people see what God can do for a man who trusts in thee."

The last part of that prayer will be our theme for the next chapter.

CHAPTER VIII

Walled Cities: Our Witness

I BELIEVE it is normal for a mature believer to want to be a good witness for Christ. However, there must be something said for the carnal believer who is really a child of God but yet has no concept of the purposes for which we are left in this world. This slight digression here is to clear the way for our main thought. For, some believers grow up quickly and may grasp the secret of the victorious life, while others may linger in the state of carnality for many years.

Joshua and Caleb had come to know, in the early stages of Israel's journey, that all their progress must be made in complete faith that only God could open the way. But all that host of Israel, other than these, seemed not to catch the secret of this mature faith. Hence, the wilderness wanderings become a display of carnality among believers.

Now, to say that these wanderers do not have any desire to witness for Christ is going a little far. There is often a desire to do God's will. This desire often becomes very active, and it is here that Satan takes advantage of them by leading them to a carnal expression of their zeal — a zeal without knowledge. Thus they substitute the works of the flesh, in good conscience, and in the zeal of religious flesh cry out, "These be the gods that brought us up out of Egypt."

However, when one has, through some experience along the way, come to a maturity of understanding that there must be more to our God than these hands can produce, however conscientious and religious we be, we come to see the failure of our witness and become dissatisfied with what we have too highly evaluated. It is then that we want a witness in keeping with our mature understanding.

While we are working in this carnal state, we may be doing more things — giving more time to church work, attending meetings, working on committees, teaching Bible classes, singing in the choir, serving on the board of deacons, and doing many other things we call service in the church — more than we will be doing when we come to a more mature grasp of the matter. Keep in mind that the carnal mind is very religious and seeks to make a satisfactory show of zeal in the eyes of the world.

My reader will not understand this if he has little acquaintance with Satan. It is our opinion that the weakness of believers in this day lies in two realms: (1) A lack of mature understanding of God, and (2) a lack of mature understanding of Satan. And the blame for most of this weakness can be laid at the door of preachers who know very little more about these matters than do the people to whom they minister. Satan deals in spiritual wickedness in high places. His is a spiritual kingdom, and he is the head of it. He works through people, just as God does, and always his method is that of counterfeiting God. The Romanist view of Satan, with horns and tail and pitch fork, is ridiculous. He transforms himself into an angel of light, is a deity himself, and is busiest where a church seeks to stand on the most spiritual ground. He works against God wherever God is working, and seeks to lead God's children into deception. Hence, he will produce a religious product, if possible, and make the carnal and untrained believer think he (the believer) is doing God's work when really he is standing in the way of God's work. The believer may be deceived into believing that this great array of accomplishments which we can chalk up on blackboards is, indeed, the accomplishments of ourselves for God. It is very flattering to the flesh to know, even though we conscientiously mean well, that we have accomplished much for God.

While the carnal believer may, at least outwardly, be busier than the spiritual believer, he will, if he ever comes to spiritual grounds, look back and see how much of what he was doing is failure. Carnal believers, who are very active in "church work" — that is, occupying positions, leading organizations, and so forth — are usually not strong on prayer, Bible study, and meditation. They are too busy. Furthermore, when and if they talk to a lost person about being saved, their witness is often hollow and superficial, with little or no spiritual impact. True they can lead a whole Sunday School class to join the church, but the product will be what much of our mill-run evangelism is today — unsaved people in the church. But when one who has grasped the secret of the spiritual speaks to the lost, there will be a solemn attention on the part of the sinner and often a serious impact on the sinner's heart. Why? It is the Spirit speaking.

Of course, the carnal believer will never see this until he has matured out of his carnality. I once heard of a young woman who was painting a picture of some modern art conception. A man who was untrained in this art looked on and said in fun, "Well, if that is an art, I am a fool." She replied, also in fun, "Well, there is one comfort a fool enjoys — he never knows it." I do not mean to reflect upon the carnal believer here, but to use this as an illustration of the fact that we will never see our childishness until we have grown up.

This is what Paul meant when he said he put away childish things (I Cor. 13). This is what the admonition to the Hebrews means (Heb. 6:1-3). Sad to say, much of our church work in this day is designed, directed, and fostered by earnest, conscientious, efficiently trained carnality. The result is very much like the modern result in education and in all other phases of our life: *it is the synthetic product administered by the vitamin process.*

But, to come to the matter of an effective spiritual witness for Christ, thank God there are those who want their lives to mean all they can for Christ. And when we have seen the dismal failure of the flesh in its work, just as we saw its failure to handle the sin question, or to bear our trials without despondency and despair, we cross Jordan and bow before the Figure in the shadows to ask again, "What sayest thou to thy servant?" The answer again is, "March around Jericho and blow the trumpet and shout, and I will tear the walls down."

Surely God never meant for religion to be as tiresome and wearying as it is to many earnest souls! There is surely a greater pathway to accomplishment in God's work than is manifest in the wearying rounds of things jamming into each other in modern church life! Do I mean less trial? No! I mean more grace and less burden.

Jesus is not boring. It is the everlasting attempt on the part of the flesh to make out a good case for Him that is boring. It is the reluctance of the flesh to give up and ride upon His grace that makes life a wearying existence. When the Spirit is in control there is love, joy, peace, and all the good fruits of the Spirit, even down in the midst of trial and burden. The Cross is not a burden; it is the only way to the source of power to lift our burdens.

And now, let us proceed. You want to be a good witness for Christ? How can you do it?

As in the realm of sin and trials, Satan will advise just what we have been discussing. But here is the best answer: *Don't try to make yourself a good witness. Yield the whole matter to our Lord and trust the whole thing to Him.* Tell Him that if you try you will make a failure and will be in His way. Tell Him you are merely a piece of clay, and that you can no more live your life effectively and for His glory than the clay can become a vessel. Withdraw from the task and rest the whole matter in His hands. Believe that He has accepted the responsibility just as you have trusted Him to do, and let it remain there for His action, not yours.

Perhaps now my reader will say: "Well, this is indeed a lazy man's religion. I am to do nothing about my sins, nothing about my trials and problems, and nothing about my witness for Christ. This is just one big glorious boat ride to Heaven, if true." Immediately doubt will set in. It can't be real, you will say. This is too easy, yea, even fantastic.

But are you not forgetting, my friend, that the battle is not in doing, but in believing? "Canst thou believe?" is ever the question. The Pharisees said to Jesus, "What shall we do that we might work the works of God?" His answer was, "This is the work of God, that ye believe on him whom he hath sent" (John 6:29). Indeed, that is a work of God. The work of God is maturing us into a faith that can take God's Word and stand on it. And this faith must be wrought in us by the Holy Spirit. It is not of ourselves, it is the gift of God. It will come to us only after we have tried the flesh and found it to be an utter failure. It will come to us only after we have been through enough of the "tribulation" to make us realize that the "carnal mind is not subject to the law of God, neither indeed can be," and that the flesh has no resource which can deal effectively with our burdens. When we become sick of our earthly gods and the efforts which we put forth to worship them, and we collapse in our helplessness upon the everlasting arms, then, and then alone, will we grasp the faith that delivers the whole matter of witnessing into the hands of God.

But how can we witness and do nothing? Here is the common error. It so happens that we will be very busy. The difference is that we will be busy in the things into which God leads us, rather than in the things which we contrive ourselves.

Now, what constitutes a good witness? We will have to be as brief as possible, for many things are pressing here for utterance. When I was a student in Greek culture my teacher asked me to write a paper on "The Hermes of Praxiteles." I knew very little of Praxiteles, and I did not study his life or history. I did study the "Hermes," a statue of a Greek god, as he conceived that god to be, and with utmost detail. I read much on the art of that time and studied pictures of the "Hermes" to see how well the artist had produced his work. It not only raised my appreciation of Greek art, but it made me very familiar with the detail in which this artist had produced his carving.

I could tell you a good deal about the artist Praxiteles, because I had studied his handiwork. And the "Hermes" was one of his witnesses to the world of art. That told others of Praxiteles.

When God has taken a sinner, born in sin, ruined in all his soul and body, doomed to eternal hell; reaches that sinner's heart with the power to believe in the blood of Christ to save; gives him the indwelling Holy Spirit; matures him through that carnal period of his life into the spiritual surrender to the will of God and, by spiritual enlightenment, helps him to reinterpret life in the light of God's grace; when He has brought that sinner to live a life as Jesus did in this world and has given him a view of it as God sees it all; He has set up in this world a carving of His own artistry that is an everlasting witness to what His grace can do for us. Is that not a good witness?

By the new birth He puts the nature of God into a child of the devil and thus begins the transformation that ultimately brings that child of Satan to be like the living God. Is not that a good witness? By the nurture of the Spirit, through trial and heartache, He makes regnant the character of Jesus in His child, and thus enables the believer to act like a citizen of Heaven in the midst of a lost and ruined world. Is not that a good witness?

What, then, is a good witness for Christ? First, a good witness must *know* Christ. He cannot know Him until he has lived with Him in places and conditions where he can learn of Christ's power and glory. This necessitates tribulation. Then, a good witness must *tell* about Christ. And how does he do this? Like the Hermes tells about Praxiteles. Though it has no voice, it speaks. And the believer is constantly speaking to this world about Jesus.

Here is a believer in whose heart God has worked, and whom God has brought across Jordan. He has love. He does not get angry when he is imposed upon, but prays for those who persecute him. Why? Because he understands something now he did not once understand. I remember a very striking case of this kind. One of my men worked in a factory with a group of cursing, wicked, lost sinners. He was the only Christian there. They made life hard for him, and he often flared up in anger and resentment. He grew to dislike these men almost to the point of hatred. He came to me about it and confessed his feeling for them. He said he could not bear it any longer. After looking into the subject, I said, "Friend, these men are not your enemies. They are the dupes of Satan. They are bound by him and blinded in their sin. Satan has them in his power, and he does not want you to break into this group with a saving testimony. If you do, some of them might be saved. So, he persecutes you through them, hoping to drive you out of the plant. Thus, he aggravates you by making them resent you and your witness to Christ. Do you not see that they are lost and in his power? As God's child, you are under great stress, but you are in a strategic position for witness. Stand there and let them curse you, but give them the witness God wants you to give."

He was a sincere Christian. He had trouble with the temper, but he saw the point. He soon came to pity these men as though they were victims of a terrible disease. And, instead of getting rid of his problem, in the Name of Christ, he assumed the ambassadorship to these men and stood in Christian spirit under their oppression. His whole viewpoint was changed. He was doing battle now with the powers of wickedness. It required prayer, and faith, and humility. Not only did it work character in Him and thus deal with some of his weaknesses, but it gave the witness God wanted there. Later on several of these men were saved. He works with them today and has their utmost respect.

How do you act while God is carving on you? If you yield and believe and let the experience be used of God, it will perform both the character of God in you and the witness of God through you. Dr. Truett said repeatedly in one of his memorable sermons, "Be careful how you behave under trial." The world is looking on to see if God is doing anything for you. Only when you are in that place where nobody else can help you, and where the flesh utterly fails, can you let the world see that there is an inner force, which is not of this world, sustaining you. Here is the witness. And when people want to know the way of God, they are going to seek the help of somebody who manifestly has been there.

Church work and the busy life of the modern church member in objective things reveal very little of the work of God in the heart. God knows that I love the brethren who have so earnestly toiled to build our modern system of activity, but it must be said in all candor that most of it can be run without prayer or deep spiritual understanding. Efficiency in the manipulation of plans and methods adapted from the world and natural abilities of speech and song and moral advisements are mainly all that is necessary to operate the modern church. In the words of a great old prophet of God which I knew in my early days, there is much "heat without moisture" in the modern operation. Good, moral, lost men are almost as useful in much that is done today in the name of religion as men of the Spirit and understanding. In fact, spiritual minds find it hard to fight in "Saul's armour," and are frequently considered fanatical and uncooperative. But when you look for the evidences of Christ in the life, they will be found in those who have suffered the scorn of this world and have walked alone in dark places with the Lord, but all the while have found "joy in tribulation." People with heart trouble will seek them for help. As long as everything is going well, the masses will move in the circle of those who are "doing things for God," but when trouble comes they will seek a cooling spring that bubbles from some isolated heart where God has been working in the night to clear the waters and make them sweet to the troubled soul.

For what is a good witness distinguished? His works, says the world. His faith, says God. And does my reader say, "Well, is it not both?" To which we answer, it is both if the faith be a faith that works, and if the works be the works of faith. The distinction here is important.

The best answer is given in the eleventh chapter of Hebrews where God memorializes what He calls a "cloud of witnesses."

In the battles of war among men, certain men are selected for what is known as a "citation." That is, the world is given notice, by certain ceremonies and symbols, that the hero accomplished an important mission under dangerous and adverse circumstances. The nearer death he came the greater the citation. And if he lost his life in the act, he received the highest recognition.

So here, the citation is for being "faithful unto death." That is, believing though it bring one to death. This does not mean that men were cited for committing suicide. It would be easy for a man to get himself killed in battle. But it means that they believed on and on unto death.

Now notice that what they are cited for is believing, instead of doing some heroic act under adverse conditions. The citation is for faith, not works. It was not for believing that God would bless what we do, but that God would do for us.

So often the kind of faith we have is a faith in our works rather than in God. This is a faith in works rather than the works of faith. The difference is immense. In the faith in works, we do *in order* to believe; and if we do not do enough, and our works do not appear to be sufficient, we do not have faith. Our faith is grounded upon our works. But the works of faith is that which we do because we believe.

For example, prayer is a work — the hardest kind of work. Now it is very easy to have faith in prayer instead of faith in God. If we pray enough and have a warm session of communion with God, we feel that our prayers will be answered. But if our prayers seem to be weak and there is lacking a warmth and fervor in them, we doubt that God will answer them. If we can pray hard enough, and feel deeply burdened, and perhaps shed some tears, we believe God has heard us. But if we cannot have this feeling, we feel that we have failed in prayer, and thus God did not hear us. But that is faith in prayer, not in God. We based our faith on our works. We should have based it entirely on God's promise that He would hear.

In revival meetings I have seen the brethren "put on the campaign" of systematic visiting and planning. When the meeting starts they may be heard to say, "This ought to be a great meeting. Everything possible has been done

to make it a success." Their faith is in their works. Often
I have seen such a meeting become what we often call a
"flop." And if the Lord does bless and save in meetings
like that, often He brings to salvation people who were
not even on the prayer and visiting lists. I know I am not
covering all situations under these statements; but if I
could summarize what I am trying to say, I would say it
this way: It is better to make contact with God before we
try to make contact with men. It is best to have our faith
in what He can do for us than in what we can do for Him.
For God is the miracle worker, and when He works He
uses His own plans and methods. All He needs is our faith.
Then what works we do will be the works of faith. Plans
and methods will proceed from Him, and they will be so
different from those we have contrived. Much of the lost
motion which nearly always characterizes our works will
be absent in His.

When our plans fail we cannot blame God. But often our
faith grows dim and we are discouraged, because our faith
was in our works instead of in our God. We set a pattern of
accomplishment and ask God to work to it. If He fails
to do that, we become confused and blame ourselves because
things did not turn out as we had hoped. "Somebody did
not work enough," we say. Or, we pronounce the whole
thing a failure because the Lord did not meet our expec-
tation and bless what we were trying to do.

This brings us to another thought about faith. Faith
does not sit in judgment on how God handles matters. I
used to worry, in revival meetings, if we did not have a
goodly number of confessions of faith. If we did have, we
all concluded we had had a good meeting. If not, we all
felt defeated and worried, saying we had not prayed enough

and worked enough. Doubtless, both were true, but that is not the real reason. Perhaps we had not made contact with God in faith before we tried to make contact with men in witness. Perhaps our prayers were asking God to bless our works instead of asking Him to give us faith. But whatever the trouble I have long since ceased to worry about "results." It is simply a commentary that God hasn't handled things as He should have. I am glad for God to use me, and I trust Him to accomplish His ends. My faith is in Him, and I leave the results with Him.

Faith is simply a witness, or a testimony, sealed by death if necessary, that the witness believes God to be true no matter how things turn out. It does not prescribe a time and manner for God to act. It leaves all that to Him and trusts on and on. And that faith is most distinguished when the circumstances and signs are most against it. I repeat, these heroes of faith were cited for believing when all was unfavorable. They are distinguished for their faith, and that is the kind of faith that works.

I have heard men say, "God helps those who help themselves." What they mean is that, if we will use our natural abilities, God will augment our resources by His blessings and help us accomplish our ends. Their judgment as to whether or not God helped depends on whether or not they accomplished their objective. Whether the statement is true or not, and we are not saying it is, visible accomplishment is not always God's objective. Visible *faith* is His end in view. He is not trying so much to produce works in us as He is to produce faith in us. God does not want to show to the world so much how we can work; He wants to show how we can believe. What He desires is that "the trial of your faith . . . might be found unto praise and honor and glory at the appearing of Jesus Christ" (I Pet. 1:7).

Don't you see, it is a glorifying faith that God wants in us? Certainly glorifying works will be the fruit of the glorifying faith, but the tree must come first; then the fruit will be quite another kind of works, the works of faith.

We must admit, again, that this is a spiritual mystery, and just everybody will not be able to see the difference. It is like the faith that saves us, so clear when experienced, but so dark to the natural mind.

In the light of these thoughts, let us look briefly at the record in Hebrews eleven. These witnesses have been brought into such dependence upon God that they do what the world could not possibly do under the given circumstances, namely, believe God. They have become acquainted with the God who "works in mysterious ways, His wonders to perform," and they do not raise questions as to what God will do or how He will do it. They simply trust the consequences to Him without knowing what He will do. They are distinguished for walking in a faith that is so unworldly that they seem to be perfectly at home in the realm of the supernatural. They get accustomed to the impossible. Through these God has revealed the works of faith, and the record is given here for our encouragement.

How did Abel witness? There hadn't been much gospel preached in this early day. It was a long, veiled look over to the cross, where the "Lamb of God" would take away the sin of the world. He did not have the abundant testimony of the Old Testament and the preaching of John the Baptist to assure him and reveal God's salvation for sinners. Any of us might have excused Abel for not understanding enough to have faith in the vague promises of a

Saviour. For look how men ignore that Saviour today, after all the revelation and preaching of the ages! Nevertheless, in humble faith, Abel brought his lamb, thereby confessing his sin and his faith in God. God sent down the fire and consumed the offering. There the matter was sealed. But it would yet be millenniums before the Saviour would come. All that Abel left with God, and his citation was for faith.

Noah's faith accepted God's word in spite of the facts that there was nothing foreseeable to prove that word; that it was contrary to all natural order or possibility; that the scorn of the world would be his for believing and declaring his faith; and that the making of an ark was such a collossal task, as well as, from all natural points of view, a very ridiculous project. He had no more to confirm his faith than what God had said, plus an hundred and twenty years to wait and see if it would come true! His citation is for faith. Is not that a good witness?

We have no reason to deal exhaustively with the faith of any of these heroes. Our purpose is to point out that in each case they believed when everything was against their faith except the Word of God.

Abraham believed in spite of natural laws. It required a miracle to produce Isaac, but Abraham doubted not. He had gone out trusting God, not knowing whither he went; he was accustomed to letting God make good his own promises without the help of the flesh. He rejoiced in the Lord when Isaac was born, for God had made His promise good. Now he can see how all the other promises concerning posterity can be assured. But just on the threshold of this great prospect Abraham is tried again. "Abraham, do you think that if you took Isaac out and gave him as an offering

to God, that God could still make good His promise?"
Abraham's reasoning was in the realm of the supernatural:
"Well, if He can bring Isaac from two bodies that have
died in their productive energies, certainly it would be nothing for God to raise him from the dead. Whether or not
He does, He commands me to slay my son. His ways are
higher than mine. I have no way of understanding them;
it is mine simply to obey."

Abraham did not know that God would stay his hand
at the execution. As far as he was concerned, he slew his
son on the altar. But when He displayed his faith, so the
world could see it (for God knew what he would do), God
held his hand and said, "It is enough." Few, if any of us,
can know what Abraham felt. We simply know that "these
all died in faith, not having received the promises, but
having seen them afar off, and were persuaded of them,
and embraced them, and confessed that they were strangers
and pilgrims on the earth" (Heb. 11:13).

It is not necessary to go on, for the Bible lists these
characters and details their works of faith. But as you
follow on, you will see that their citation is for their faith,
and a faith that has everything against it but the Word
of God. This is what constitutes heroic faith.

Does anybody think it is easy to take God at His word,
when everything else is against it? If we can come back
to the God of miracle, it may be. But we will have to have
a better acquaintance with that God than is current among
us if we are to see Him display His works in our behalf.
For we are more accustomed to having faith in our works
than in God. How many times we have heard men say, "If
we can get everybody working together in this or that
plan, we can do great things for God!" But such a zeal

brought us to faith in works for God rather than in the God who works for us.

The battle is between two gods — our God and Satan. Our God deals in the resources of His own power, while Satan deals in the resources of our flesh. And if Satan cannot draw us completely away from our God, he will lead us to show our devotion to Him through the efforts and energies of the flesh rather than through our faith in the power of God. This inevitably leads to the substitution of our ways for God's ways, and brings us to a faith in our works rather than in God.

And how did we come into this state? We failed to keep separate from the world. In our zeal to "make a success out of God" by encompassing large numbers of followers for Him, we lowered the walls of separation and let the world come in. The God in the cloud was too slow for them. They could not "wait on the Lord," so they began to cry, "Make us gods that we can see." Thus we turned to our own hand-carved substitutes, the machinery and devices of the flesh; and here we are! Larger numbers than ever before, but less power! Progress minus purity! Profession minus power! Efficiency of the flesh minus fruit of the Spirit! And on and on!

O that we might come back to the God who can help us! How we need Him, right now! And who else can help us? It is our hope that the trials of these days will bring that faith to the front. For that faith is best revealed under trial. That is why God lets His children walk in such places.

We might never have heard of Daniel if he had not been thrown into the lion's den. Nor would we have heard of the God which Daniel declared in his faith. All this could be said for the children of the fiery furnace. Also for

Job, who, in his darkest hour, cried out: "I do not see God before me nor behind me; on the right hand nor the left; but He knows the way that I take." That solved the case for Job. Thus God had a chance to say to Satan, and to all the world, "See, he trusts me!"

God has faithful ones today, too. Once a good woman was dying with cancer. In her days of health she had witnessed to the lost. Now she was brought low, waiting to die. A lost man who had a high regard for her, but who did not understand her faith, sent her a message asking her to go and see a "faith doctor" who reputedly could heal cancer. She had me write him a letter in which she said in part: "I appreciate your kind interest in my welfare, and I pray that God will bless you for it. However, you do not understand. It is not important that I get well; it is only important that I do God's will. He has let me live for some purpose of His own wisdom; it may be that He will heal me. But, it may be that He wants me to die, for some purpose still known only to Him. Whatever He chooses, I must yield myself to His good pleasure. If faith will heal, I have the faith. We will use every means of medical aid that God has provided, but the outcome is entirely with Him. I would not try to deprive Him of doing with His own what He wills. Should I get well of this disease, I must die at last of something else. Being healed is not the greatest thing in life; being His is the greatest realization of any life. If I die I am sure He will in my death perform His will just as much as He would in healing me. As for my pain, He will supply grace for every hour, and in it will reveal Himself to me more tenderly. While I suffer, He will be able to show the world about me that I still love and trust Him, and in that way my witness will be more convincing. Meanwhile, I hope you and others will see how blessed it is to be in the hands of One who will see to it that all things work together for good to them that love God. I pray that He may soon be able to count you in that number. He will be with me every moment. I trust Him fully, and I know His grace will be sufficient. Thank you again, and may God bless you!" She died believing. How can you make a better witness than this?

So, the summary of it all is this: "Have faith in God." In all the experiences He permits in your life, no matter what they may be, He knew it all the time and will be ready for them when they come. In your trials He will (1) become to you a greater God, and (2) He will through you reveal Himself to others. And all your trials and sorrows will be sanctified to that purpose if you trust Him. He is a greater God who can sustain you there than is He who can remove your trials. Praise His Name!

CHAPTER IX

Consecration and Crucifixion

WE COME HERE to study the method of God more closely. I am indebted here especially to a work called *The Law of Faith,* by Norman Grubb, for help in clarifying some of my ideas.

I have, through the years, had a fashion of trying to impress my hearer with this statement: In the light of man's judgment, God is usually slow and awkward. He never does anything with the finesse that is characteristic of man's work. He resorts to means and methods that are often very foolish to man and goes in such a round-about way to do His work that it is wearying to the flesh. People who work in the energy of the flesh have little patience with, or confidence in, God's ways. That is why we substitute for God's ways the efficiency of the flesh. That is why the product of today is so often synthetic.

What it all means is that God is doing so much more than we are doing, it is difficult for us to see why He does it the way He does and why it takes so long. Only men of faith can expect His methods to succeed or can have the patience to wait for them to mature.

Furthermore, there is so much misunderstanding as to the aims and ends of God's purposes, that we find hosts of people working for things which God does not seek nor foster. This, however, is too involved for this book, and we will simply leave the statement for the reader's reflection. But it is true that a clearer understanding of the aims and objectives of God would serve to concentrate our blunderbuss efforts on the main things and save a lot of lost motion.

It takes a long time for God to grow a tree, or cut a deep river gorge, or grow a man or a woman; and the greater His work of art, the longer it takes. We must remember also that it takes a long time for God to grow a Christian into maturity, and the means by which He does it are quite involved. For this reason we should never get ahead of God nor sit in judgment on His methods.

For instance, young people are often asked to consecrate their lives to God. When I first heard that invitation, I wanted to do it. But after I did what I thought was consecration, I expected God to lead me into some unusual expression of spiritual life which would make me very effective. When it finally dawned on me that doors were not opening into any spectacular field of expression, I wondered why, and was somewhat discouraged.

I was converted up the creek in the old church, where meeting time was once a month, and where a weak little Sunday School was held only during the summer months. Revivals came along as God seemed to indicate. We never planned revivals; we simply met for the meetings of the church on Saturday and Sunday once each month, and, if the Spirit "moved" during the meetings and the brethren were impressed, we had meeting the next night. If the Spirit "moved" again, we announced meeting for the next night. Often a revival would break out, and many would be saved. I have seen these meetings go on for three or four weeks, and the Spirit moving to make people happy and bring many into the fold. The testimony that arose from these meetings was, "The Lord has blessed us." Here it is again — what the Lord did for us. Yes, it kept us right busy, for we had to tell of His blessings and let others know what the Lord was doing for us, and that attracted lost people from all over the country. They came and saw what our God was doing for us and were impressed, convicted, and saved. That is the way it will have to be now if we ever reach the lost. We will have to give God a chance to do something for us.

Having been reared up in that kind of religion and being an eye witness to the character it produced in the lives of those who were saved, it is natural for me to think that it could be done that way now. During one of these meetings I was saved. I remember how I came to see that I could do nothing, and, in blind trust, I fell upon God's Son as my hope. Faith, given by God, laid hold on the Word of promise, and the defence rested with a plea of guilty. Jesus saved me! I did the best I knew how to grow in grace, taught a little Sunday School class, prayed God to call me to preach, and served in whatever way I could. One day while I was hoeing corn around a sunny point, my mind was filled with thoughts of God. It was there that I heard God's call. There was no soft organ playing, other than the breeze; no choir but the birds; no consecration meeting, nor superficial seance with the Holy Spirit. Just God talking to His child in a setting wholly lacking in the soft light, soft music atmosphere of modern consecration meetings. There I eagerly answered His call.

I cannot detail the life which followed. I went to a mission school for high school training, then to a Christian college. As I see it now, I was often sinful, often conceited, often ambitious, but I thought I was humble. There seemed to be no spectacular success in my ministry. I plodded along with the usual life of a boy struggling through unwise days, but with a desire to grow better and more effective. After college I started in a completely organized modern church as director of its educational activities and its music. I was irked by the endless details and the lack of spiritual power. Modern churches seemed to be nothing to me but big business institutions. Everybody was busy, working feverishly at something, and yet I could not see the end. The theory seemed to be that if you will set the mill up in order and get all its parts coordinating, it will, of itself, do a mass job of log sawing. The only lack seemed to be in the difficulty of getting steam in the engine and logs on the carriage. Well, I was a failure there and resigned. Nobody was to blame but myself. I just couldn't reconcile this big modern church life with the way the Spirit "moved" at the old home church.

I continued to preach wherever I had opportunity. I married, went through some bereavements and other sorrows, had some reverses financially, and at last landed in my present pastorate twenty years ago. Through these years Satan has been on the job. But through these years I have come to understand the matters written in this book.

The outstanding discovery of my life is the difference between consecration and crucifixion. Here I wish to discuss this matter, for it is most important.

Consecration, or dedication, or whatever it is, is merely the start of spiritual growth. I had thought it would be the beginning of a spectacular and phenomenal spiritual success. Really, I see now that my first acts of "consecration" had been merely an expression of a desire to live closer to God. That is usually what it means when people respond to such invitations. It was not until I came to study God's Word in the light of the deeper spiritual life that I came to know the meaning of dedication of life. It cannot be done again and again. It is once for all, just as Jordan is crossed once for all. It is, simply, arriving at maturity. There God takes over and, from there on, your life is under His direction. You may be inconstant and often forget, but God does not. Just as we trust Him to save us and He takes complete responsibility from there on, so, when we trust Him to take our lives and make them successful, He takes over and begins to work His purposes in us. He must do something for *us!*

This is *absolute surrender.* You are troubled about your sins and failures; you hand that over to Him. You are harrassed and burdened with trial; you hand that over to Him. You want to be a good witness but find you are helpless to do it; you hand that over to Him. The whole life is surrendered to Him, and from there on He is responsible to take the lump of clay and make of it what He will. You learn, by experience, to follow the course of faith we have been discussing in previous chapters. On all these points you learn to trust God and see Him do for you what you found you could not do. Every stronghold is overcome by faith.

Keep in mind what it is to overcome by faith. It is *not to remove sin,* but to believe what the Bible says, that you are not under the rule of sin now, but under grace. Therefore you will not be dealt with as a sinner under judgment; the judgment of sins has passed for you. You will be dealt with now as a son under grace. This you *believe,* and are free from the reign of sin. You are in the hands of a loving Father — a Great Physician who has taken your case and promises to cure you. This victory is *not to remove your trials* but to make something out of them. And, in so dealing with your sins and with your trials, you will find God so good and so gracious, and His wonderful ways so far above anything the world has to offer, that you will stand through trial with grace in your heart and show what God can do for you. You will be so happy to be associated in this intimate walk with God, and will be so full of the spiritual understanding which all this brings, that your mouth will be open and you will be eager to tell "the wonderful things of God." This will make you *a great witness*.

But when you dedicate your life to God, He accepts you as a lamb for the slaughter. You are an offering for the altar. Like Jesus, you are to be "kept up" until you are proven. That is, you are to be put through the tests of tribulation and patience and all the steps God may use to prepare you for the offering. Then you will be asked to go on the Cross and die with your Lord.

Consecration is merely giving yourself to God so that He can crucify you. It is the crucifixion that puts you where you can become useful. If Jesus had merely lived in this world, though He lived perfectly, that would have been no help for lost sinners. That was a test of His obedience and perfection to qualify Him for the offering. The Cross is what made Him valuable to us. And you and I may be entirely dedicated to God, but He will have to put us on the Cross before self can be put asunder so that we can be entirely His. This age talks much of consecration, but it knows little of crucifixion.

This is the pattern of life for all of God's saints. I should like to take Moses as a classic example. Moses made a spectacular dedication of life to God. He "chose rather to suffer affliction with the people of God than to enjoy the pleasures of sin for a season."

When you consider what Moses was giving up and the prospect of the people of God there in bondage, it seems indeed a spectacular surrender. If Moses had come into our services then, we would have introduced him and have made a long speech about what he gave up to serve God. He would almost be worshipped because of his "sacrifice." I always get a little nausea when somebody goes to telling what somebody gave up to serve God. Poor God! what a beggar He has been! Nothing to offer anyone, but just has to beg people to give up their rich and glorious life here to serve Him because He is so pitiful and has nobody to help Him! But that is the world's estimate of this world and God's heritage.

Nobody can make any sacrifices to God. Whatever we give up cost God His precious Son. Let no one be so irreverent as to think we have anything to offer Him. He is self-sufficient, and no one can give unto Him. All we can do is worship Him, and that means utterly to deplore ourselves and confess that we deserve nothing but to go to hell, and that He only is worthy to live. That is worship! People often weep more over the hardships of the missionaries than they do over the lost condition of the heathen to whom they go. You can get more money by appealing for the comfort of a missionary than you can for the salvation of a lost sinner. All credit to those who serve God in these fields. But nobody ever outgave God. We have nothing to sacrifice. We simply have the choice of entering into His purpose and saving our lives by losing them, or of losing them by withholding them from Him.

So, Moses made the surrender. No doubt it was genuine. But like many of us who have done this, he set about immediately in the wisdom and energy of the flesh to do great things for God. So, Moses went out immediately to set things in order for God's people. You know the story. He saw an Egyptian task master beating an Israelite slave. He killed the task master, and set the Israelite free.

Now, we are made to wonder if this was the way God wanted him to approach his task. Of course, the symbolism here is that he identified himself with his people and was rejected, as Jesus was later on. But there was something more involved. There is a sense in which it was a mistake for Moses to begin, in the energy of the flesh, to deliver God's people. The next day he saw two Israelites fighting and sought to make peace between them. They turned upon him and accused him of slaying the Egyptian. There is much preaching in this incident, but suffice it to say now that Moses was trying to solve the problem in his own wisdom. The symbolism is full: there must be a crucifixion before Israel can be delivered. So, by the turn of events, Moses is driven into the land of Midian, where God can prepare him for his great task.

And of what does that preparation consist? Simply, crucifixion! Moses was no doubt very earnest and conscientious when he went out to relieve his people of their burdens, and do all he could to deliver them. However, he went in the energy and wisdom of the flesh and got exactly nowhere. This is the way so many earnest souls try to serve the Lord. They have seriously dedicated their lives unto God, now they feel that God should begin to use them mightily. They are instructed to give their talents and abilities to God, and let God use them in a great way. So often they are disap-

pointed because they do not know the body which is conse-
crated is then to be crucified.

It is so easy for us to act in the wisdom of the flesh,
because we are earnest and conscientious. Here is where
Satan takes his advantage. He meets the conscientious
soul with a proposition of the flesh, and makes it seem to
have come from God. It is so easy for Satan to make our
idea seem to be the very one God has sent. One wonders
how many of us would have been fooled by the opportunity
Moses had as the son of Pharaoh's daughter. I can hear
some preacher advising the young man: "Moses, you love
your people and want to serve them, don't you? Well,
God has given you the greatest opportunity any man can
ever have to deliver them. You remember how God directed
your parents to place you where the daughter of Pharaoh
could find you. Then how God delivered you to her, and
you became a prince in Pharaoh's kingdom. Do you not
see the hand of God in this? You just stay in there until
Pharaoh dies, then you will become king. Then you can deliver your people. It is a made-to-order plan from God, and
one can plainly see that this is His will."

We wonder why Moses did not do it this way. It is so
appealing. And sensible! But the foolishness of God is
wiser than men! God is not seeking our information; He
is seeking our identification. To have the inside track on
the government would have been the direct route to the
deliverance of Israel. Why did God have to go forty years
out of the way, and on a long sojourn in the land of Midian,
when He had such a direct route to the objective? Well, the
answer is, "As the heavens are high above the earth, so are
my ways higher than your ways." If Moses had done it
that way, he would have gotten the glory. So, God just

goes so far out of the way and waits so long, that nobody could say it was a smart plan of human ingenuity. Besides, God had to have a crucified man through whom to deliver Israel, and He had to take him out there to the Cross. He wanted Moses to become identified with Him, not with Egypt; so that when the deliverance came it would be from God, not from some smart human strategist. All God wants with any of us is our identification with Him; He has plans of His own.

Well, Moses has struck in the energy of the flesh and suddenly finds himself sitting yonder in Midian minding Jethro's sheep. I imagine he thought he had made a mistake, but that it would soon "blow over" and he could return to carry out his work. At least he has time for sober reflection. He can't see why it turned out this way. He was well equipped to do the job. He was trained in all the wisdom and customs of the Egyptians and knew the strategy of government well. He could make great speeches, and his princely background in the Egyptian world ought to have made him a dead ringer for the role of Israel's leader. He imagined, no doubt, how he could sway them when he let some of his brethren introduce him, and tell what he had given up to identify himself with them. The glamour of his former life would be no obstacle to the feminine element of Jacob's descendants, though he would let that have its greater power by a sort of subtle obscurity. Earnest as he was, like most of us, he no doubt was willing to place all this fine equipment at the disposal of God, and for the blessing of his people.

I do not reflect upon the sincerity of Moses nor upon that of any of our people who dedicate their lives to Christ. But I do say that many people never reach that state of maturity where they can discover how much actual self there is in what they do. There is nothing in the flesh but something to crucify. In Galatians 5:19 we get a picture of what the flesh can do: "Now the works of the flesh are these; adultery, fornication, uncleanness, lasciviousness, idolatry, witchcraft, hatred, variance, emulations, wrath, strife, seditions, heresies, envyings, murders, drunkenness, revellings, and such like." If these are the works of the flesh, no wonder it has to be crucified! Human strategy is usually wrong, for God is working from above, and we are working from below. Our viewpoints are entirely opposite; why should not our methods be so? No wonder God's ways are so different from ours!

Moses has been in Midian now a year and has been courting one of Jethro's daughters. Nothing more has come of the Lord's plan to deliver Israel. By now Moses feels, no doubt, that there was some mistake in the whole thing. He settles down to marriage and begins living there for the rest of his life. Ten years pass, and he is quite settled in Midian. He has grown rusty in court manners, has settled into the customs of the Midianites, smells like wool, and only occasionally reflects upon the brilliant prospects that lay before him on the day of his dedication to God. Who knows what went through his mind? I am merely imagining. But something of this nature entered into his reflections as the years went by. Ten years of this kind of life, wondering what God meant, and why everything turned out this way for a man who so earnestly dedicated his life to God, is certainly enough to puzzle the most faithful of God's children. Elijah grew despondent in a few hours of reverses. So have others.

Twenty years gone by! Connections in Egypt have about died out. Wonder what is going on in that country now? How are God's people faring? Will He ever raise up anybody to deliver them? Thirty years — long years — go by. No evidence of God reviving His interest in Moses. A shepherd of Midian with a little family goes on toward his eightieth year, and life in Egypt becomes now only a faint memory. Nobody knows how far from the culture of Egypt these years have removed Moses. Plans and dreams and enthusiasm of youth now mock the venerable man. Aspirations have fallen, and for all He knows God has forgotten. Forty years have covered the pathway back to Egypt, and there is no thought of ever retracing his steps. He is too old now, and life has settled down toward eventide. What church would have called Moses as pastor now?

Suddenly a little way from him there is a bush on fire. Now God speaks. "Worship! God is here! Put off your shoes; this is holy ground!"

Moses draws near in reverence, heart beating with awe and wonder. "I want you to go and deliver Israel," says the voice. I can hear his heart throbbing. His brow wrinkles, and he tries to remember. "Deliver Israel!" he repeats with astonishment. Then, with probing memory, he repeats slowly, "Deliver Israel!" The third chapter of Exodus gives the account. After much conversation we come to the fourth chapter where Moses files objection. They will not believe him! God takes care of that with a sign. Then Moses remembers how well trained he was forty years ago, and how well equipped he was to do the job. But now — now he is out of date. He has lost his culture, his manners of court, his appeal to the children of Israel; he cannot speak now with convincing power as he once did. He has lost his talents!

This is the confession God is waiting for. In substance He says, "Well, Moses, this is the time I have been waiting for. You started out to deliver Israel with a very earnest spirit. But you had your mouth full of things you were going to say and your head full of things you were going to do. You didn't let me fill you with my words and my thoughts. You wanted me to use what you had, but that would not serve my purposes. It has taken forty years for you to let your words and thoughts die out, so that I could fill you with mine. Now that you are empty of self, and recognize the fact that you have no power or wisdom with which to do God's work, I am ready to take you and fill you with divine wisdom and power. I have waited until you died out so I could get in you and deliver Israel. It took forty years to crucify you until you confessed yourself dead. Now that you realize you are inadequate, I will fill you and make you powerful in the Lord. From now on, when you go to the great task to which I have called you, instead of uttering your speeches, you will say to Pharaoh, "Thus saith the Lord!"

We all know the story from there on. Moses made his consecration at the age of forty; God finished his crucifixion at the age of eighty. Now he was ready for the Master's use. And so it is with us all. We are long on consecration, and do it over and over. We are not afraid of that. But we dread those nails that pin self on the Cross. It takes a long time to crucify self. Yea, we will ever have to be driving another nail in our hands, for as long as Satan can have access to the flesh, self will want to come down from the Cross. But if we are to save others we must stay up there. It was a great Christ who could have come down from the Cross, but it was a greater Christ who could stay up there. Self must get out of the way if we are to serve God, and the only place for him is on the Cross. Until then he will always be in God's way.

This is the pattern of the lives of God's saints, Abraham, Jacob, David, Elijah, Peter, Paul, and all the rest. Consecration is not enough; we must go to the altar and die. That is why it takes God so long to bring us to maturity and fruitfulness. This is the difference between the carnal believer and the spiritual believer. The carnal man may dedicate his life to Christ, but he is unwilling to go to the Cross. The spiritual man knows the meaning of the Cross in his life. He pins the wisdom of self to the Cross and accepts the wisdom of God.

When Thomas said, "Except I see the nail prints, I will not believe," he was expressing the attitude of this world toward God's children. Only when lost men can see the marks of crucifixion in us, and can see that God has given us a life that is not of self, will they be impressed with our God and believe.

CHAPTER X

How to Make the Surrender

I BELIEVE the best way to tell my reader how to make the surrender to a life of faith is to tell how it came in my own life. He will doubtless be surprised to find that it is no startling event, no phenomenal experience, no "second blessing" of any sort. It was just a growing up, or coming to maturity of understanding, and beginning to live in the spiritual mind.

Let me remind the reader of something I have already said: Spirituality is not necessarily goodness. It is, rather, a spiritual understanding, which brings us to see that we are not good, can never be, and that God alone can do for us what is needful to our spiritual growth and achievement. Thus we turn it all over to God, and walk by faith, trusting Him to work His work in us.

This maturity may be illustrated. We have all heard of that period in a young man's life which we call "climbing fool's hill." That is the time when he is learning so much and so rapidly that he is sure he will know everything in a short while. He cannot take advice, knows more than anybody else, sees the out-modedness of anyone who dares to advise, and climbs the steeps by leaps and bounds. It is as if he had started at the Atlantic coast line, rapidly crossing the narrow plains that lead to the mountains just a little to the west of the ocean. By leaps and bounds he comes to the highest peak, in all the enthusiasm of his young manhood, expecting the world to crown him for his success. When he arrives he is startled to see that this is merely the beginning; that soon he must level off to the long trek down into the basin of the Ohio river and out across the miles and miles that lead to the plains west of the Mississippi. Farther on in the blue distance arise the mighty Rockies over which he must pass before he can slip down to the sunset of glory which life at last can give.

Of course, he cannot see all that lies ahead of him, but he now becomes seriously aware of the fact that life is too long and too involved to try to walk alone. Soberness sets in, and he begins to search for a guide who can lead him along that way. He looks back now and sees many a misstep which he could have avoided if he had listened to more mature guidance. He begins to be aware that it is better not to walk alone.

This is the feeling that came over me several years ago, and I felt deeply the need of some one who knew the way to guide me. I became aware of the fact that I could not walk this way alone. I began to seek the guidance of God more seriously. I was a young pastor, with great church problems. There were deaths in the family, births of our two babies, financial difficulties, and many other problems combining to make life burdensome and uncertain. I looked back, like the boy on the mountain top, and saw many mistakes I had made. I had not known how to live, how to manage, how to be a good father, a good husband, a good pastor, how to use my time, and a thousand things I did not know. Like all men who come to some maturity, I have wished a thousand times that I might go back and change some of my mistakes. I knew so little about how to live. And on that basis I must realize that even yet I know so little about it.

I wanted to be a good servant of God. I longed for power and wisdom and godliness. I fought testings and temptation and found myself so weak and powerless, so often failing. I made such a light impact upon the world around me. I came to see my nothingness and prayed daily for light and help. I wanted to be wholly my Lord's but seemed not to make any progress in that direction. Dozens of things combined to irritate me and to make my progress impossible. I was bound by cords. When I would do good evil was present with me. I found a war in my members, the flesh warring against the Spirit. Earnestly I cried for deliverance.

Let me say here, dear reader, you can never know the life of faith unless you want to know it. You have to have the desire, or it will never come. And this, it seems, must come from God. It does not arise from the flesh.

God was helping me, but I didn't know it. A little book dropped into my life now and then. Usually, the little books are best. I wish this one were smaller. Even now I think it is getting too long. But, I say, a book came now and then, with a message urging my surrender. Over and over I surrendered. I did not make public consecrations; I just prayed God to help me find the answer. I believe that the more I prayed and sought help the more there was to irritate and make me sin. Temptation kept growing instead of decreasing. I was reading the Word, reading spiritual messages in books or articles, making a complete surrender every day, and looking for results, but seeing none. Every day it seemed that I had less results to encourage me. I was not spiritual, and I knew it. I saw by the results that

I was making no progress. There was too much sin, too much perplexity, too much weakness. I did not know what to do.

That lasted over a period of several years. I was so unwise in my attempts to direct my own life and the life of my family, and that of my church! I can look with great embarrassment upon the mistakes I made. The only thing I can remember that makes me feel grateful was this: I was saying all the while, "Lord, I am making such a poor showing. I am ashamed that I can be no better and do no better. I want to be all you want me to be, but I'm failing by the hour. I may never succeed, Lord, but one thing I know, and that I can die with — I *want* to be yours and I *want* your help." I believe if loved ones could have looked into my heart during that struggle they would have seen a different man on the inside from the one they some times saw outwardly.

Then one day a little book came into my hands. I will tell you the name of it, for it may help you. It is quite well known. It is, *The Christian's Secret of a Happy Life,* by Hannah Whitall Smith. I don't remember much that is in it, though I read it several times. There was only one little spot that I needed badly.

I shall state merely the substance of what the author says in the chapter on "How to Enter In." She said, in substance: "You have often come to Him, bringing your life in surrender. You have wanted to be His completely and feel the power to live the risen life. You know He wants you to live that life and offers you His grace and power with which to live it. But you looked for results and it did not seem that anything came of your surrender. Here is the thing you failed to do: you failed to believe that He took your life when you gave it to Him. You came offering your life, but you did not believe He took it. Why didn't you? Did He not invite you to trust Him with your life? Did you not do it? Is He not bound to take it and make of it what He wills? Then believe it, and leave it there."

It was so simple when I saw it. It was exactly what they had told me to do when I was saved. God had spoken, they said, now I was to believe His Word and take it as true. After I trusted and was saved, it all seemed so simple. Now here I was with a life I couldn't live, and crying out for somebody to help me. Christ was saying He would take my life and do with it what He would. I had surrendered it to Him, but *had failed to believe that He took it.*

The Holy Spirit helped me to grasp this simple truth, and put me over the hurdle. I began to accept it as done. For a long year I watched for results. Nothing happened, except that maybe I was weaker than ever. I think now God was testing my faith. Every time the question would arise, and no results were there to confirm me, I would say, "Lord, I trusted you; if you are true, you took my life. I cannot live it; you must do it for me. Regardless of the fact that I seem to be making no progress, I am leaving it where I put it. From now on what happens to me is your business and your responsibility. I have trusted you; I will leave it there, even if I never make any further progress in spiritual things."

A year and a half passed before I noticed any change. I did not know what to expect, whether a great experience or — well, what? I just didn't know. I did have some faint idea that God would make me powerful to sway the people in my preaching. I was willing for it all to be to His credit, and I had no thought of counting on self for anything, but I thought perhaps God had some great work for me to do and might lead me into it in time. I wanted to be used mightily. Speaking modestly, I did not think I was too poorly equipped with abilities as to render me hopeless along this line. I thought of a bigger church, a larger congregation, a more powerful message, and a wider sweep of my ministry as the years came. I hoped for some definite usefulness along this line. But I humbly waited on God and asked Him to choose for me.

An occasional book dropped into my life along the way. These and bits of experiences from others enlightened me and helped me to find my way. One day it began to dawn on me that I was possessed with a sort of tenderness toward Christ that I had not noticed before, and a burden for lost people began to increase. Also a patience with God's children who sin and err along the way of life. The pastoral heart began to grow in me. It was not the earthquake, nor the whirlwind, nor the fire. It was just the still, small voice. I cannot explain it other than to say there came a settling of life, a deeper flow, a peace that God had things in His own hand and that He would do what He wished with His own.

Then one day there dropped into my reading a little tract. It was small and almost unworldly. I shall quote it here, though I am sure many have read it. It had a tremendous meaning to my life. The title of it is, "Others May, You Cannot." It says:

"If God has called you to be really like Jesus in all your spirit, He will draw you into a life of crucifixion and humility, and put on you such demands of obedience, that He will not allow you to follow other Christians, and in many ways He will seem to let other good people do things which He will not let you do.

"Others can brag on themselves, and their work, on their success, on their writings, but the Holy Spirit will not allow you to do any such thing, and if you begin it, He will lead you into some deep mortification that will make you despise yourself and all your good works.

"Others will be allowed to succeed in making money, but it is likely God will keep you poor because He wants you to have something far better than gold, and that is a helpless dependence on Him, that He may have the privilege of supplying your needs day by day out of an unseen treasury.

"The Lord will let others be honored and put forward, and keep you hid away in obscurity, because He wants to produce some choice fragrant fruit for His glory, which can be produced only in the shade.

"God will let others be great, but will keep you small. He will let others do a work for Him, and get credit for it, but He will make you work and toil on without knowing how much you are doing; and then to make your work still more precious, He will let others get the credit for the work you have done, and this will make your reward ten times greater when He comes. The Holy Spirit will put strict watch over you, with a jealous love, and will rebuke you for little words and feelings or for wasting your time, which other Christians never seemed distressed over. So make up your mind that God is an infinite Sovereign, and has a right to do as He pleases with His own, and He will not explain to you a thousand things which may puzzle your reason in His dealings with you. He will wrap you up in jealous love, and let other people say and do many things that you cannot do or say. Settle it forever, that you are to deal directly with the Holy Spirit, and that He is to have the privilege of tying your tongue, or chaining your hand, or closing your eyes, in ways that others are not dealt with. Now, when you are so possessed with the living God that you are, in your secret heart, pleased and delighted over this peculiar, personal, private, jealous guardianship and management of the Holy Spirit over your life, you will have found the vestibule of Heaven." —(Selected)

I have never known the author of this, and I think it has been published by different publishers, but it has been in my files for several years, and has helped me in many dark hours. Be assured, dear reader, "It is not as though I had already attained, either were already mature; but I follow after . . . ." I have not the slightest idea that God would ever include me in this select group, but the content of that little tract has helped me to trust when I could not understand.

I have said in the earlier pages of this book that when a Christian makes a real surrender — that is, when he crosses Jordan — he is in the land of the giants. Instead of expecting ease and comfort now he must expect war. He is no longer a babe in Christ, but a soldier of the Cross. He will find that "this vile world" is not "a friend to grace, to help him on to God." He is now in the land where the battle is against "spiritual wickedness in high places" and the weapons of our warfare are not carnal, but spiritual. It is the "good fight of faith" and we are to have our faith tested at every round. It is a walk now from one situation to another, with opposition at every turn. Lion's dens and fiery furnaces and Goliaths will be ever in our pathway. Carnal weapons can never oppose them; it is a fight of faith.

Somewhere vaguely I had preached this truth. Maybe I had picked it up from reading, or, it might have been so plainly written in the Bible that I could not help but find it there, even though it did not occur to me out of experience. Anyway it lingered vaguely in my memory. But I had no idea how fierce the reality could be in experience. And that brings me to a pause — a sacred pause — where twelve years of memory begin to roll before me. Those who know my life will understand if I do not give the details. Others will wonder. But still, it is not different from many another. Perhaps a little difference in the way we have dealt with it all, but everybody has trouble. The only question is its purpose in our lives and what we do with it.

When God takes over the life of His child, as I have indicated here, He often takes that child down into a dark cavern where diamonds lie; or out into a lonely wilderness where all is quiet but the voice of God. He does not do His best artistry before a world that will not understand. He has business with His child which must be done in the inner sanctum, and the details of His artistry are not seen — only the finished canvas. For this reason I cannot discuss further the experiences of my life. They do not amount to much, in the first place, and whatever they mean to God and to me, I cannot presume to think they would be important to the world. A little later I will give a few conclusions about it all.

CHAPTER XI

The Place of Prayer

WE CANNOT close this study without saying something about the place of prayer in the fight of faith, for everything depends on this. If anybody thinks this is a lazy man's religion, and there is nothing to do, let him start here. In all my ministry I find fewer people who want to pray than any other kind. It is the hardest work in the world, the most neglected, and the most important.

Prayer is turning on the power. I remember when I was a small boy my uncles owned a saw mill. I worked for them some, cleaning out the sawdust pit. I have seen them work for days setting up the mill. The boiler would be anchored, the saw rig set, the carriage and track set up, and the big belt put on. All the little necessary touches were finally finished, and we were all called to positions. The steam would be popping out the pop valve, and the gauge registering power. At a given signal the engineer would open the throttle, and the big belt would leap into action. The large circular saw would go whizzing around, while the sawyer pulled his lever and the carriage moved up with a big log against the saw. Things would begin to take place then. Everybody was moving as slabs, lumber, and cross-ties fell from the carriage. There was work going on. Every part of that machinery was so tied together that the steam power could drive it into action. It had to act!

Now notice. No matter how much machinery, nor how well it was set up, there was no work going on until that steam hit the pistons. And I believe that throttle is prayer. The only time work is being done in God's people is when spiritual power hits our hearts. And that means, when we are praying. A praying people are a working people. They have to work! Power from on high drives them. And prayer is the throttle God has put in our hands which sets the power working in our hearts. When we pray, we open the pistons of our hearts, and that power rushes in to fill us with faith. Faith is absolutely dependent on prayer. A prayerless people have no faith. A praying people have faith to remove mountains.

Of what does good praying consist? (1) Worship. That includes a feeling and expression of humility which denies the flesh any recognition or merit whatsoever. It sets God on the throne of the heart, acknowledging all good from Him alone, confessing ourselves to be utterly sinful and wretched and needy. It deplores everything but God. That is worship. (2) Contemplation of God. This is why it takes time to pray. This, too, is worship, but it serves a purpose in our lives. What I mean by the contemplation of God is to take in the size of God. David had done this; that is why he knew God could slay Goliath. Daniel had contemplated God's power. And so on. It is good to get the correct size of God, else our faith will be small. With the works program of our modern day we have reduced God to a small household affair, so that we don't expect much from Him. Let me give you some examples of prayer from those who have taken in God's size. And when they pray they go over these things to remind themselves that they are not praying to a little God. That enlarges their faith. The Psalms are full of these prayers.

In the 46th Psalm, for example, the writer is in need of refuge and help in trouble. He says, "God is our refuge and strength, a very present help in trouble. Therefore will we not fear, though the earth be removed, though the mountains be carried into the midst of the sea." On he goes expressing faith in God's power to stand though everything fall. Then look in the eighth verse. He says, "Come, behold the works of the Lord." Then he tells what desolations the Lord has wrought. Read these verses and see how he builds up His God to a mighty being. Then he quiets himself by saying, "The Lord of hosts is with us; the God of Jacob is our refuge." When you pray long enough to take in God's size, you generate faith.

You find this kind of praying through all the Old Testament. Now take a classic example from the New Testament. Look in Acts 4:23-30. The disciples have been in a terrible spot. I have an idea that many of us, being let go, would not have contemplated a return trip to the front of battle and would have prayed the Lord to give us another field. But they bolstered up their faith by contemplating the size of God again, as they prayed: "Lord, thou art God, which hast made heaven, and earth, and the sea, and all that in them is . . ." Well, when you get hold of a God that big, He ought to be able to handle the situation. But this was a part of their prayer — reminding themselves how big God is by reciting a few things He had done. And this helps us to have faith — this contemplation of God — and it ought to be a large part of prayer. (3) Resignation to the will of God. Not trying to get rid of our problems, but trying to fit into the will of God. This is yoke walking. It will require constant bending of the neck, and yielding of the body, and inconveniencing the fleshly mind. It will set aside many of our plans and connections and desires. It is constant dying — continuous dying. "We are accounted as sheep for the slaughter," so we ought to yield to the Cross. Letting God have His way all the time is hard on the flesh, but we can't have faith unless we do it. When we put things in God's hands we know it will be all right, but it takes praying to put them there. The flesh will rise up for battle, and push in for recognition of its plans and desires right while we are praying. We have to work hard on our knees if we get the faith that is the victory. That is the only place we can deal with the flesh, the ground of prayer. Paul knew this. When he gave us all the armour in Ephesians 6, he starts us fighting on the ground of prayer. The first action is praying; for there we deal with the flesh, and when we have put to death the flesh and get it out of the way, we come up with faith which is the power that drives the mill and makes things happen that man can't do any other way. Then, (4) prayer is asking God, as the Spirit prompts us, and receiving the answer in whatever way God chooses to answer for our good. Many a request from a child is answered, but denied. We must always leave to our sovereign God the advisability of answering by granting what we have asked. But if we ask according to the Spirit, we can be sure of the request being granted. However, this develops into a longer discussion than we are able to give here.

Much more could be said about prayer, but our reason for bringing the matter to attention here is to emphasize the thought that prayer is the place where faith begins. This is the first work of the believer in any service to God. If we cannot pray, nothing else will happen. If the believer will not pray, he cannot have faith; and if he have not faith, our Lord can "do no mighty works" because of his unbelief. His God will be reduced to his own size, and nothing more than what the flesh can do will take place.

That is where the modern church is working, all too often, now. We cannot have faith without opening the heart valves so that the power from on high can come in. And what, again, is that power? *It is the power to believe God* and *expect Him to tear down the wall!* This is a mystery to most people, I know, but here is the deep secret of the supernatural, and it is as simple as saving faith. Yet it is just as difficult for the believer as saving faith is for the lost. Not the power to do, that is not what we need, but the power to believe that God will do. And this comes by praying the heart open to God so that the power to believe will come in. For faith is the victory!

CHAPTER XII

This Is the Victory

I AM conscious of the fact that I have repeated a great deal in this book. I have done it because I have feared my reader will miss the emphasis. I do not underestimate the intelligence of those who read; I merely question the ability of the author to make himself clearly understood. This truth is so buried beneath the handiwork of modern churches that we are likely to miss it in the most manifest portrayals. Hence, if my reader has tired of repetition, charge it to my zeal for this truth to be known.

I am also conscious of the fact that I have discussed many angles of the believer's life, and some may remark that I have tried to deal with everything in one book. But what is there of a spiritual nature that is not connected in some way with this life of faith? Besides, there is much in my heart yet that I would like to put in this volume, but I have refrained in order not to be tiresome.

Now, in the hope that I shall be able to clinch the truth with a personal testimony, let me bring it to as hasty a conclusion as I can. I submit it humbly, guarding against any undue exploitation of my own experiences, and because my reader has a right to know how faith has worked in my own life.

I am coming to the close of my twentieth year in the present pastorate. It is not, nor has it ever been, a large pastorate. The church is small and struggling. I have never been recognized as any great personality anywhere. I am just one of the thousands of plodding pastors buried in the small fields of our land, going on in face of great opposition both in the church and out, but trying to be faithful where we are called.

About two years after I had given my whole life over to God and started leaving everything to Him, I soon came to see that God was not to lead me along the highway of great accomplishment. He was going to take me into the storm where I could learn of Him. I had trusted Him to lead; now He was leading.

My experiences are not singular; many a life has been shattered by sorrow. I was preaching a life of faith; now I was to see if it worked. Without giving details, let me say that one of life's great tragedies fell across my pathway, and in a manner which brought me great anguish and embarassment. For a year I saw it coming. I submitted the matter to God in prayer and believed that He would prevent what was threatening. I was often informed of prospective events, but I did not believe they would finally come to pass. I lived on with the secret bottled up in my heart, working as if nothing were wrong, believing that God would intervene at His own time and bring me victory. I was sure that, while He was driving me to my face in humility and confession of sin, He would break through the cloud in time to save me from utter darkness.

Result? The event transpired on schedule. I was plunged into great sorrow and embarassment. I lived only one day at a time, trying to conduct myself as a believer, feeling sure that God would, out of the wreckage, bring glory at last. I then began to pray for restoration of order in my life. I was sure now that God could put things back together, and out of it all would shine His glory. I prayed and believed and expected, but He did not do this. Then, there was one more event in prospect which, if it came to pass, would complete the wreckage and doom any hope of restoration. I set this before my God and prayed and believed that He would not let this take place. It, too, came to pass on schedule.

Humbled as I was, God gave me nothing I had prayed for, and I was stunned. It took some time to recover from my shock. All the while I was going on with my work as pastor, but my heart was like lead. I had preached to others that if we prayed for something in faith, God would grant it. I still believe that is true, but sometimes God deals with us in exceptional ways for His own sovereign purpose. We must learn to trust and follow His will as He reveals it day by day.

After I had humbled myself more and had prepared to fold up my ministry and retire to seclusion, if that seemed to be the way God wanted it, I put my aching heart before the Lord and leaned upon His breast like a hurt child, "snubbing" out my sorrow and asking my Father to tell me what was wrong. I was saying, "Lord, I preached it to others, and I believed it. And when I tried it, it hasn't seemed to work. All that was dear to me is gone, and the whole thing looks so utterly contrary to what is favorable to your cause. I was willing to be chastened; I deserved that. But I am confused about faith, and I don't know what to say. If I cannot demonstrate what I have preached, I want to know what is wrong with my understanding. I am so confused, and my heart is aching."

As I mused, and leaned upon His breast for succor, thoughts came to my mind. He seemed to say: "Yes, my child, you humbled yourself, you prayed earnestly, and believed, as you had told others to do. You counted on me to do just what you asked, and you wanted it for my glory. I failed to answer your first request, then your second, then your third. And then, as you thought, all was over. Your loss was complete. I allowed Satan to bring complete wreckage to all that was dear to you. In the first place, that is the way this world is set up, and, except for the grace and power of God, that is what would happen to all men. But you — you are mine! Suppose you did not have me? I gave up my all for you. And, by so doing, I have been able to save you and others. I know it looks hopeless to you, but is anything so bad that God cannot bring something out of it? Is it not in the most impossible situations where God's work shines most brightly? Leave the wreckage to me. It may take a long time. You may be called home before it is finished. Didn't you start out by trusting me with everything?"

Then I felt a whimpering "yes" pressing for expression. I gave assent. Then he continued, "Faith is not trusting God to get something; faith is trusting God when there seems to be nothing left. When everything is gone, with no hope of restoration; when there is nothing on which to base one's faith; then, *can you still trust God?*"

Now I had met the test. I took stock of my faith. Thank God it had not occurred to me to quit believing Him. So, hurt as I was, and leaving all the wreckage to Him, seeing no way that it could be restored, I said to Him as I lay my head again on His breast, "Yes, Lord, I still believe." It was only a thought in my mind, but it came as quickly and as clearly as if He had spoken, "Then, my child, you have the victory!"

Through years of preaching I had quoted that verse in John's letter many a time, "This is the victory that overcometh the world, even our faith," but here for the first time in my life I got its meaning. It was so simple I was ashamed that I had not seen it before. Unconsciously, I had preached that if we trust God our faith *will bring* the victory. But now I saw that it rather says, "Faith IS the victory!" And that is what the old song says, too, but I hadn't seen it before. So, it is not when you get what faith is asking for, that you have the victory; it is when you have faith, though everything be denied, that you have victory.

Does God give answers to prayers? Certainly, and often something better than what we are asking. But we must always leave that to Him. One thing we must remember, He did not come into this world to quiet all the storms, nor to heal all our diseases, nor to set aright all the tangled relationships of our lives, nor to relieve all our heartaches.

And if we have that faith we can sing:

> "*We have an anchor that keeps the soul,*
> *Stedfast and sure while the billows roll;*
> *Fastened to the Rock which cannot move,*
> *Grounded firm and deep in the Saviour's love.*"

One day He is coming to lift us out of this stormy deep; to take us from troubled seas to peaceful shores. And it does not matter if the storms blow hard, and there is wreckage all around, we must demonstrate to the world that Christ holds us steady and serene through it all. We must believe when there is no earthly reason to believe. That will tend to cause other people to forsake the false securities of this world and attract them to the faith which penetrates the sureties of Heaven. And whether or not God puts together, by a miracle *for* us, the pieces of our battered ship, we must believe so as to let them see the miracle of faith that He has performed *in* us — that faith which believes God in spite of everything. And in so doing we shall, after all, let them see God's miracle *through* us. This IS the victory, even our FAITH!

And is my reader curious as to how it works ten years after trial began? The battle goes on.

"Temptations, hidden snares, often take us unawares,
And our hearts are made to bleed
For many a thoughtless word or deed;
And we wonder why the test, when we try to do our best,
But we'll understand it better by and by."

I have never become a sensational success. Good brethren have said to me, "Your life is like a book. Why don't you tell your story as a testimony?" Then I have had men speak, in order to accentuate my labors in the Lord, of what I could have done had I traveled with the world. To me this is absolutely asinine from a world viewpoint, and blasphemy from God's viewpoint. I get sick at heart when I hear men praising men for their great accomplishments. When we get to talking about what men have given up to serve God, I grow pale with fear. Who has anything to offer God? Who can make sacrifices but God? Everything we have is sinful and we are utterly depraved. What can we give Him but the consent of our wills to let Him enrich us with His own treasures of grace?

Tell my story? What is it but shame and misery and wretchedness? Who of us has a story that is worth telling? There is but one Hero! There is but one story to tell, and that is the story of Jesus and redeeming love.

In my own eyes I am a greater sinner than I ever was before. I believe this is because "mine eyes have seen the King." I am weaker today, in my own eyes, than I ever was before. I believe this is because I have felt His power. I will never be a hero now; only Christ can be that. I will never shine nor be recognized as a great light in this world; for the light of His glory has blinded my eyes to the tinsel glitter of this world. I seem to have a continual decrease of what I used to think of as my talents and abilities. I have no idea of the accomplishments of my feeble ministry. To me it is a constant failure, for I see what He has done.

I rejoice when people who are in trouble, especially "heart" trouble, come to me for help. Maybe they think I understand. But I am not popular. I am constantly criticized, both in the church and out. Like all men, I long for more evidence of success, but God knows what I am doing, and why. He needs men everywhere. As far as I am concerned He has me here.

I cannot emphasize too much that no one will find any aspects of a super-man of faith in me. We have a tendency to "glamorize" people who talk as I have written. Those who come to know me will be disappointed in the living example of what I say. Like Elijah, I am "a man of like passions" such as others, and in my own estimation I am a total failure of what a man of faith should be. I grow restless, at times irritable, have all the little complaints that are human, and am afflicted with moods that drive me to the juniper tree. I often languish under the gourd vine and the flesh is ever knocking for admittance into my sense of self pity. I grow lonely and feel the simple desires of human life as much as all others. I am introspective, feel now the immodesty of using the personal pronoun "I" as I have in this book, but feel that it is necessary for this personal testimony. All I say is to accentuate what God has done for me, not what I am doing for Him. By that I mean that, in spite of what I am, He is still glorious. No one need be surprised at what I may do, erring as I am, but I will always have a glorious and perfect account to give of Him. And that is what He has done for me.

Then, is there nothing to do but "be carried to the skies on flowery beds of ease?" Yes, there is much to do. I am always tired. By the time I use my opportunities to preach and tell the things I have written in this book, I am mighty busy. And, by the time I have waited on the Lord, still believing, and have told by word of mouth *what God has done for me,* I have the feeling that I have done what He *really wants me to do for Him.* For thus the world has seen *faith working!* Indeed, THIS IS THE VICTORY!